MW01626394

This publication was made possible through the generous support of:

The City of Joliet Mayor Arthur Schultz and members of the Joliet City Council: Joseph Shetina, Timothy Brophy, Anthony Uremovic, Alex Ledesma, Warren Dorris, Thomas Giarrante, Jan Quillman, and Michael Turk.

The City of Joliet sponsored the sculptures and mosaics depicted in this book. Additional financial support for the Jesse Barfield Sculpture and the George Mikan Sculpture was provided, in part by Wadsworth Golf Construction Company. The following provided general financial support for Friends of Community Public Art: Samuel and Kathy Anderson, Caterpillar Foundation, Columbian Agency, Joliet/Will County Center for Economic Development, Joliet City Center Partnership, First Midwest Bank, ExxonMobil, Frank and Sue Turk, Richard and Marcia Pauling, the local labor unions and the members of Friends of Community Public Art.

Friends of Community Public Art is partially supported by the Illinois Arts Council, a state agency.

sculptures

The Great Columns of Joliet

By Friends of
Community Public Art

Distributed by the
University of Illinois Press
Urbana and Chicago

This book is printed on acid-free paper. Printing/Binding: Verona, Italy

Friends of Community Public Art
310 North Ottawa Street
Joliet, Illinois 60432-2513

Complete Cataloging-in-Publication Information is available from the Library of Congress
Friends of Community Public Art, Inc., 1996
ISBN – 10: 0-252-07441-6
ISBN – 13: 978-0-252-07441-7

Publisher: Friends of Community Public Art
Project Directors: Kathleen Farrell, Kathleen Scarboro
Art Editor: Kathleen Scarboro, Kathleen Farrell
Literary Editor: John Stobart
Copy Editor: Faye Andrashko
Production Manager: Chantele White
Fiscal Manager: Karen Lega
Photo Editor: Kathleen Scarboro, Kathleen Farrell
Photographers: Kathleen Scarboro, Terri Lesnak, Kathleen Farrell
Writer: Friends of Community Public Art, Inc.
Designer: Toby Zallman, Z...ART & Graphics

Front Cover Art: Kathleen Scarboro, Jesus Rodriguez, Saul Chavira, Sarah Furst, Kathleen Farrell
Back Cover Art: Kathleen Farrell, Kathleen Scarboro

Contents

Acknowledgements 7
Foreword 8
Introduction to Friends of Community Public Art 10
Introduction to Poetry 12

history

1 **Building the Lincoln Highway** 14
Concrete Rivers
2 **Route 66: The Mother Road** 16
Route 66
3 **Veteran Women: Proudly They Serve** 18
Joliet's Female Veterans
4 **Sator Sanchez: World War II Hero** 20
Sandy Sanchez
The Story of Sator Sanchez 22
The Story of Katherine Dunham 23
5 **Katherine Dunham: Dancer, Choreographer and Citizen** 24
Madame Dunham
6 **George Mikan: Changed the Game of Basketball Forever** 26
Goaltender
7 **Jesse Barfield: A Great Joliet Baseball Tradition** 28
Joliet's Jesse
8 **Community Policing: Working with Citizens for a Safer City** 30
A Policeman is the Semaphore of Civilization
9 **Joliet Fire Fighters: Helping Hands, Caring Hearts** 32
Firefighter
10 **Monarch of the Prairie** 34
The Bison's Alimony
11 **Asakiwaki Woman** 36
They Endured
12 **The First Pioneer** 38
Progressive Pioneer
13 **1850s Barber: Underground Railroad Hero** 40
Together From the Start
14 **Traveling the Plank Road: A Working Companionship** 42
Founding Father
15 **History Clings Like Ivy** 44
Cathedral Area
16 **Historic Preservation: Our Neighborhood** 46
Rejuvenation
17 **Portals of Buell Avenue** 48
Dark Good Memories
18 **The New Steelman** 50
Steelman 2006

nature

19 **Egrets in the Wetland** 52
Egret
20 **The Barn Owl and the Moon** 54
The Barn Owl and the Moon
21 **Red Tail Hawk: The Nature of Our Neighborhood** 56
The Hawk

22 **Fox in Cattails** 58
Hail, Splendidissima!
23 **Nature: The Flow of Life** 60
The Flow

allegory

24 **Wisdom: A Grandmother and Grandchild** 62
Touching
25 **Mother Nature** 64
Cold Spring
26 **The Tiller of the Earth** 66
The Tiller of the Earth
27 **Spirit of the River** 68
Spirit Sonnet
28 **The Boy and the Rose** 70
By Any Other Name
29 **An Informed Mind Can Make Better Choices** 72
An Informed Mind
30 **Justice** 74
Conviction
31 **Ebb and Flow** 76
Think Even This
32 **The New Dress** 78
The New Dress
33 **The Gift of Music** 80
New Horn

education

34 **I Wonder (Meadowview Elementary School)** 82
I Wonder
35 **A Teacher's Gift (Sator Sanchez Elementary School)** 84
Bombardier Martyrdom
36 **High Expectations (Washington Jr. High School)** 86
High Expectations
37 **The Creative Spirit Soars (Grand Prairie Elementary School)** 88
The Ponder Bird
38 **Reaching for Our Destinies (Plainfield South High School)** 90
Reaching for Our Destinies
39 **Education is the Window to the World (Dirksen Jr. High School)** 92
March Madness: Intergalactic Gravity
40 **Planting the Seeds: Children and Education (Taft Elementary School)** 94
Child Guide
41 **Alice: Phyllis Reynolds Naylor's Young Heroine** 96
Alice on a Book

Artists photographs and resumes 98
Poets photographs and resumes 100
Map of Sculptures 106
Photographs of Columns 108
Selected Resource Guide 110
Index 111

Acknowledgements

Friends of Community Public Art wishes to acknowledge the generous financial support from the City of Joliet. We wish to thank (bottom left-right) Alex Ledesma, Mayor Arthur Schultz, Jan Quillman, (back row left-right) Timothy Brophy, Warren Dorris, Thomas Giarrante, Joseph Shetina, Michael Turk, and Anthony Uremovic. FCPA would also like to thank from the City of Joliet: John Mezera, City Manager; Jim Shapard, Deputy City Manager; and Jim Haller, Director of Community and Economic Development, all from the City of Joliet.

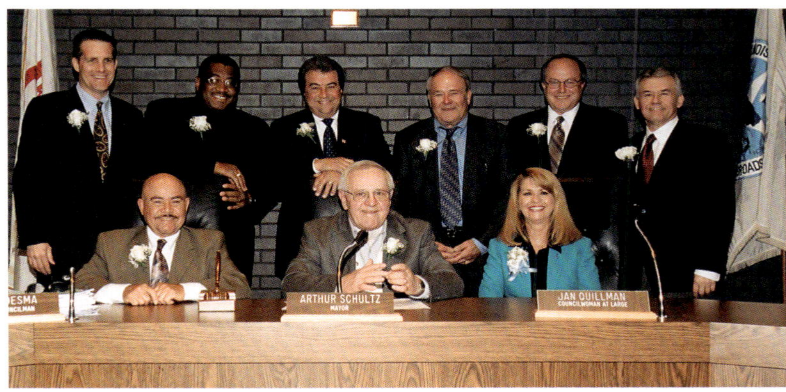

Photograph by Larry Kane

Joliet City Council

Community Public Art is an intensively collaborative effort. Many individuals and organizations provided information, photographs, or other materials to our lead artists. They include Joliet Area Historical Museum, Lincoln Highway Association, John and Lenore Weiss, Route 66 Association, American Legion Post #1080, Joseph Belman, Phyllis Reynolds Naylor, Joliet Public Library, City of Joliet Police Department, City of Joliet Fire Department, Cathedral Area Preservation Association, Clarice Boswell, Hope Rajala, Rita Renwick, Sunnyhill Skilled Rehab Center, Vicki Perella, Jean Howard, Patty Cranmer, Judge Gerald Kinney, Judge Kathleen Kallan, and Isle a la Cache Museum. FCPA would also like to thank the many models who generously gave their time to pose for our artists to capture their faces, hands, or bodies in clay. They include Hannah Lingafelter, Karina Mora, Meg Starasinich, Michael Hunger, Leonard Thompson, Ignacio Salazar, Al Patterson, Elise Nygard, Consuelo Orazco, Hunter Gallaher, Nina Crudup, David Ellis, Darchand Myer, Jesus Rodriguez Jr., Allison McSherry, Jackie Schuldt, Austin Perella, Alyssa Wilderman, Sophia Lopez, Vanessa Reyes, Kenneth Haywood, Adam Theile, Mira Weisenthal, Adam Umek, DeAndre Redmond, Jamie Biederman, Crystal Aguilar, and Michelle Lega.

The Public Art program would not be complete without the community outreach in education, dedication celebrations, exhibitions, fundraising, column locations, and media coverage. In addition to the City of Joliet, FCPA would like to thank other organizations and individuals who provided invaluable assistance. They include Joliet/Will County Center for Economic Development, Joliet City Center Partnership, Joliet Visitor's Bureau, 3 Rivers Construction Alliance, Joliet Park District,The Billie Limacher Bicentennial Park, Bonnie Winfrey, Yvonne Brittian-Whitlow, Jayme Cain, Carolyn Tate, Beverly Williams, Frank Stewart, Generation Dance, Nicole Clark, Theodore Jameson, Ruby Streate, Roxy Fuqua, Lynn Lichtenauer, JTHS Alumni Program, JJC Alumni Association, Joliet Dodge, Remco Medical, Harrah's Joliet Casino, Rialto Square Theatre, Katherine Dunham, The Missouri Historical Society, Joliet Jackhammers, NAACP, Joliet Grade School District #86, First Presbyterian Church, Joliet Township High School District #204, Forest Preserve District of Will County, Plainfield Park District, Troy Grade School District #30-c, Joliet Jewish Congregation, St. John's Lutheran Church, Westfield Louis Joliet Mall, Joliet Region Chamber of Commerce; Plainfield School District #202, *The Joliet Times Weekly, El Conquistador, Herald News*, WJOL, Rebecca Lantka, Ann Hintz, Jim Smith, Rev. Genevieve Brown, Maria Cisneros, Tom Manley, Barb Gutierrez, and Michelle Greuling.

FCPA would like to acknowledge the following organizations for their generous donation of time, supplies, and/or expertise for the creation and installation of these sculptures and mosaics: Pullara Construction, Welsch Red-E-Mix Concrete, Serena Concrete Construction, Ceramic Tile Layers and Terrazzo Workers (IUBAC), Bricklayers and Allied Craft Workers (IUBAC), Greenscape Services Corp., Glen Schulte of Joliet Junior College, Corsetti Structural Steel, PT Ferro Construction, Lindblad Construction Company of Joliet, Bizazza Tile, Pete Georgeopulos (The Fence Doctor), Unit Step, and Albarran Fine Services.

And finally FCPA would like to thank Ruth Modric for her expertise on printing.

Foreword

Kathleen Farrell

How it started

Ancient Persian columns, topped with sculptures of massive bullheads, inspired the first sculpture-column proposed to the City of Joliet. *Egrets in the Wetland*, which features two egrets atop a nine-foot-tall mosaic-covered concrete column, emerged from this concept. This was the beginning of an ongoing, fruitful collaboration between FCPA and the City of Joliet in developing a sculptural identity for Joliet while also creating an enriched sense of community.

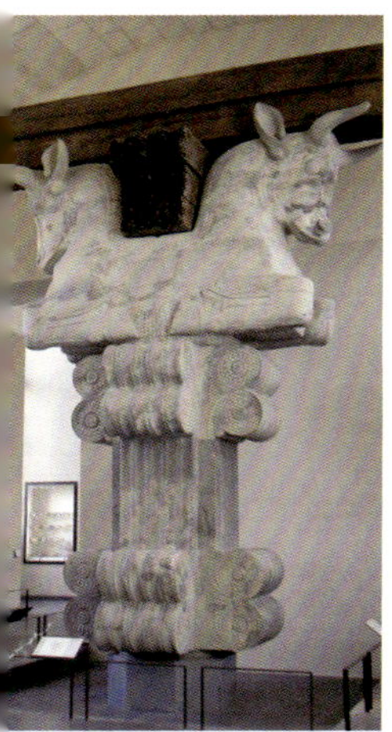

A bullhead-topped column from the Palace of Darius in Susa (Iran) constructed in late-sixth-century BC.

In 1994, following a recommendation from a professional design consultant, the City of Joliet built two "identity columns." These limestone, steel, and glass columns were placed in downtown Joliet. To me, the idea that a specific type of art object could appear repeatedly throughout the city and become recognizable as a Joliet icon was very exciting. In 1998, I suggested that the city and FCPA create identity columns that featured original sculpture and hand-cut mosaics. While costing less than the limestone and steel columns, the FCPA's proposed sculpture-mosaic columns would create original art and employ local artists. The city's funds would be spent in town, thus supporting the local economy. Because many neighborhood sites had little pedestrian traffic, placing sculptures on columns would make it possible for relatively small, low-cost sculptures to be visible from a distance, especially from moving cars. The city agreed to the proposal, and District One Councilman Joe Shetina, using Neighborhood Improvement funds, commissioned FCPA to create the identity column *Egrets in the Wetland* for the entrance to Rock Run Wetland Park, located in his district.

The creative process begins

As in a Renaissance art studio, FCPA artists work in groups. FCPA senior artists Kathleen Scarboro, Tom Manley, and I analyze the needs of the community and suggest topics and locations for the sculpture-mosaic columns. Sometimes the community, city council members, and city officials assist with suggested topics and locations. These topic categories include history, nature, allegory, and education. As did her predecessor, Marcia Pauling, FCPA administrator Chantele White coordinates with the lead artists on the details of community meetings, in-progress photography, news releases, license agreements, column installation, sculpture and mosaic installation, and dedication celebrations.

FCPA's sculpture-mosaic projects always begin with public meetings and the forming of a committee to work with the artist and the city. As part of the community public art process, FCPA hosts artist design sessions, where newer artists work with lead artists in suggesting design options for a project.

The representational and allegorical style of the sculpture-mosaic columns reflects FCPA's dedication to making Joliet the "Florence of the Midwest." Our lead artists frequently look to Classical Greek, Italian Renaissance, and Baroque sculpture for inspiration in producing dynamic poses. Other favorite sources of inspiration are traditional Hindu sculpture, the work of Auguste Rodin, and contemporary figurative and abstract sculpture.

The artisans: division of labor

The work on the projects is divided into four categories: senior artist, lead artist, armature maker, and assistant artist.

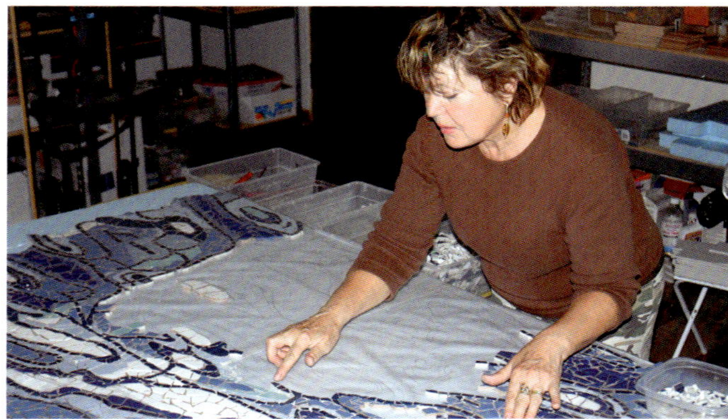

FCPA Lead Artist Sharka Glet works on a broken-tile ceramic mosaic.

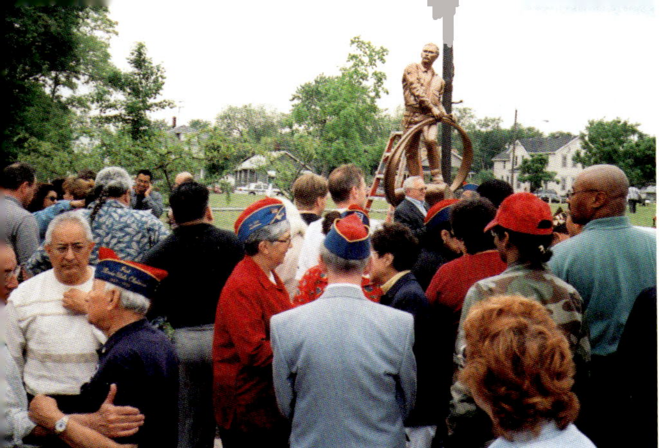

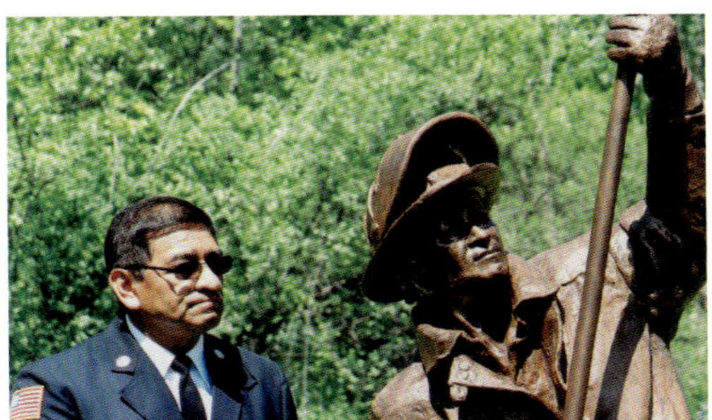

TOP Sator Sanchez WWII Hero dedication ceremony.
BOTTOM Fireman Ignacio Salazar poses with sculpture of his image.

The **senior artists** suggest sculpture and mosaic topics and locations, supervise the work of all other artists, and develop strategies for the future direction of FCPA. Senior and lead artists must be able to produce strong, realistic work, as well as have the vision to create original compositions with content understandable by the public.

The **lead artist** designs the sculpture or mosaic, forms the community committee, and researches the project's topic. Upon approval of a concept from the city and the community committee, the lead artist then creates a scale model. The sculpture scale model is made in oil clay or wax, and the mosaic scale model is painted on canvas. Once the scale model has been approved, work can begin on the life-size sculpture or mosaic.

Building an armature, or framework, initiates the hot- or cold-cast bronze sculpture process. The purpose of the armature is to provide support to the modeling material so its major structural elements won't deform during the modeling process. Sculptor David Standifer recently joined FCPA's Dante DiBartolo in creating armatures for our sculptures. First, the **armature maker** projects life-size photographs of the scale model onto paper. He then plots the size and placement of the armature and creates it out of steel or wood, adding flexible aluminum pipe and wire so the artist is able to move the arms, legs, and head positions of the sculpture. The lead artist works with the armature maker, adjusting the position as necessary. Then polyurethane foam is sprayed on the armature, in the shape of the finished sculpture. After the polyurethane has hardened, the foam is carved into a shape roughly resembling the dimensions of the finished sculpture. Because clay is very heavy, using a foam core helps reduce the weight of the finished sculpture.

Often the lead artist has **assistant artists**. In sculpture, they help apply oil clay to the foam-covered armature. The lead artist supervises the assistant artists throughout the process. On other occasions the lead artist hires an assistant artist who is particularly skilled in detail work or lettering. After assisting on a number of sculptures and developing strong figurative and representational skills, assistant artists can become lead artists.

Once the lead artist has completed the oil clay sculpture, it is either delivered to the foundry for hot-cast bronze casting, or to the fiberglass fabricator for cold-cast bronze casting. Although the FCPA artist's work is identical for both processes, products of hot-cast bronze cost more than twice as much as those of cold-cast bronze.

"Art is not a mirror held up to reality, but a hammer with which to shape it."

—Bertolt Brecht

The dedication ceremony

Most sculpture-mosaic columns are unveiled at a community celebration. Community committee members working with the FCPA administrator organize an event that frequently includes bands, choirs, and refreshments.

After the initial success of FCPA's first sculpture-column, the City of Joliet and councilmen from all five districts have continued to commission this type of work from FCPA. As of 2005, the city has sponsored 41 outdoor community-based sculptures, 35 of which are based on the original "identity column" concept. Three more are in the works for 2006, further expanding Joliet's unique approach to creating a visual identity for the community that depicts and celebrates the lives of the local people, their history, and their hopes for the future.

Introduction to Friends of Community Public Art

Kathleen Scarboro

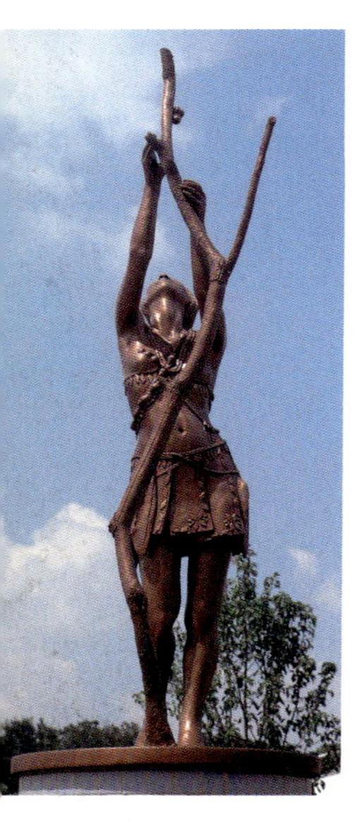

FCPA was formed to be an artist-run, multiracial, intercultural organization. The goal of FCPA is to maintain a core group of professional artists who have developed the technical and organizational skills to make site-specific, audience-responsive work. Nurturing a dynamic dialogue between artists, community members, and local government, FCPA creates bridges of communication between all partners, which ensures the appropriation of artwork by the community as a whole. FCPA firmly believes that the existence of public art and its support by the population are symbols of the vitality of the inner impetus toward fulfillment within a society. The role of public art is to take the aspirations that give meaning to people's lives and to translate them from a latent impulse into physical form to be shared and used as a source of continued inspiration by all.

Public art changes people's attitudes towards art in general. A large percentage of most populations consider art to be simply a form of decoration that can be omitted with no particular loss; art is seen as superfluous. As we form our committees at FCPA, in order to communicate with the various segments of the population, we make evident to people that the ideas we develop in our works can be the very ideas they consider fundamental to their philosophies as teachers, historians, or urban planners. When they realize that a work can take on subject matter like environmental and historical issues, they realize its true power as a communication tool. It becomes clear to them that artworks enhance the urban environment and deliver powerful and pertinent messages to the population.

We live in a time of growing uniformity. Everywhere we look, we see the same modular architecture, the same chain restaurants and department stores. Public art based on the history and experiences of a specific population allows us to once again appropriate our urban environment. It creates an opportunity to make our cities resemble us specifically. And of course, if the art is of high esthetic and technical quality, it changes the image of the city itself. A certain refinement appears, so that even a passing traveler immediately realizes that this city has invested in quality of life, has made the effort to create a rich, interesting, and visually pleasing urban environment for all to share. Such a city will develop a reputation that will attract newcomers who appreciate these efforts, and who will, in turn, make their contributions. It will also attract tourists who can come and enjoy the visual wealth, thereby generating economic growth.

Even a brief look at world history over the centuries illustrates the vital link between the artist and the societies they represent. We understand diverse civilizations by studying and enjoying the great works of art and literature that they have created. It is a relatively recent (less than two centuries old) and local (western Europe and North America) phenomenon that so many contemporary artists find themselves outside society, deprived of the means and capacity to assume their historical role as a voices for the beliefs and aspirations of the populations to which they belong. This unnatural situation can change if certain measures are taken. Our public art policy and this book are measures that FCPA believes will help to remedy the current problem by revitalizing the link between poets, historians, artists and their communities.

By combining poetry, history, and visual art in this project, FCPA hopes to create a situation in which these three disciplines can mutually enhance the understanding and enjoyment of each other. Collaboration among poets and visual artists produces a desirable effect; by placing two artistic disciplines together, people more sensitive to one of the art forms will automatically be exposed to the other, helping them to become more aware of another mode of expression.

After determining that this book would be about both sculpture and poetry, FCPA contacted one of our members, John Stobart, and asked him to be the literary editor for this work. A search for local poets was undertaken, and the poets were invited to look at the sculptures that already existed, or were in the process of being created, and to choose the themes with which they felt an affinity.

Some of the poems are totally adapted to the sculptures; others use the sculpture as a suggestion or point of departure. The poets' responses to the sculptures were always surprising, creating new interpretative possibilities.

The subject matter of the sculptures was determined by consulting our various partners: city planners, teachers, historians, and neighborhood associations. Sites and subject matter were chosen in order to give the maximum benefit and visibility to a maximum number of people. Many of the sculptures are placed near schools in order to help children to learn about the arts and to be used as tools by the teachers. In all of our sculptures on the theme of education, we try to help children to realize that we believe in them as the future of humanity, and we consider their potential to be unlimited. The historical sculptures honor distinguished citizens who came before us and, through their exemplary accomplishments, enriched our lives. The goal of all the sculptures is to contribute to the creation of an urban environment worthy of the subtlety, awareness, and creativity, of the human spirit.

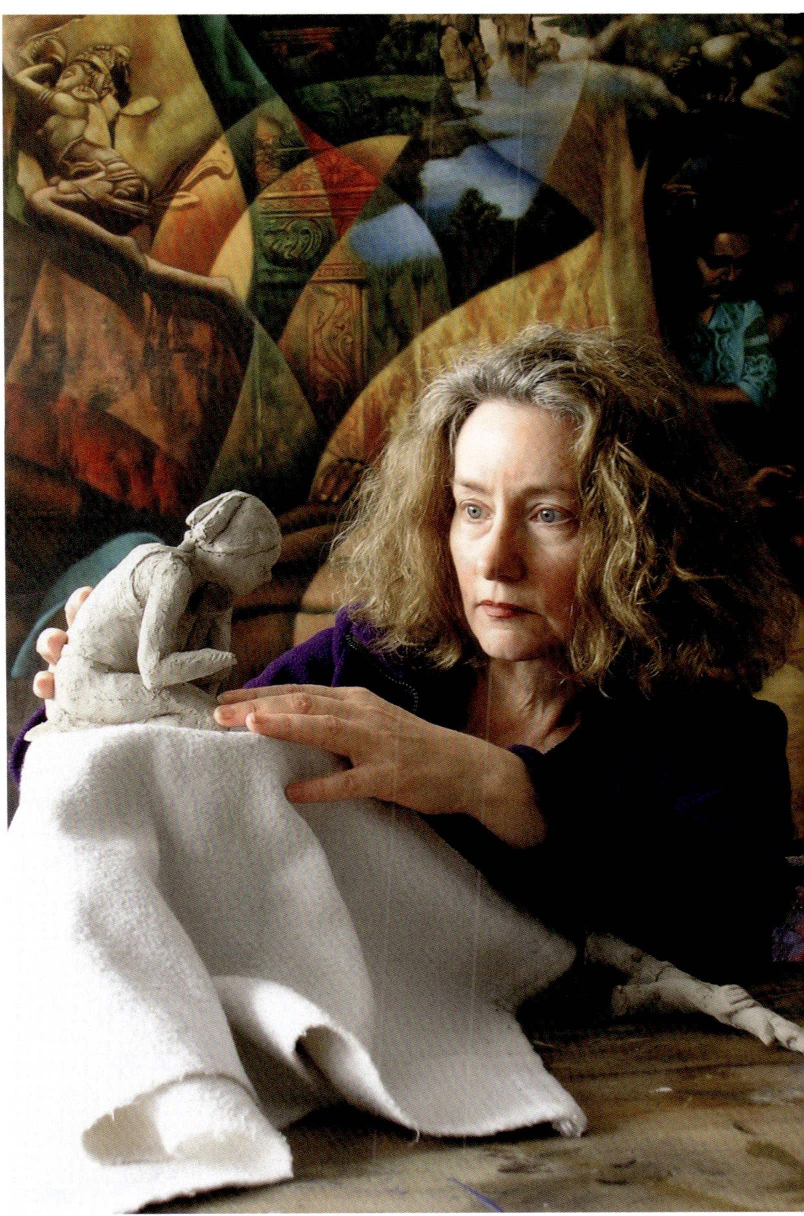

Kathleen Scarboro works on her sculpture in her studio.

Introduction to Poetry

John Stobart

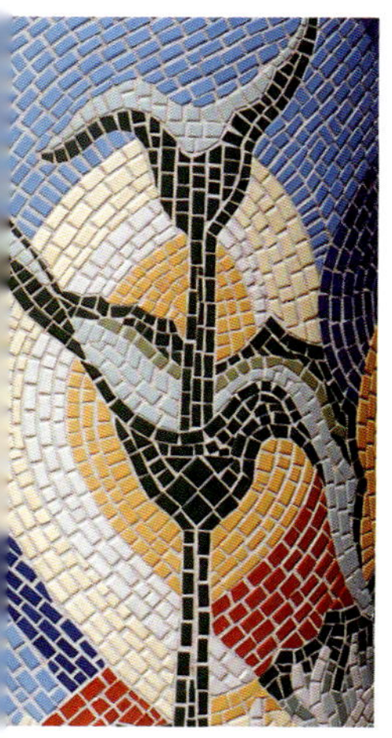

The poems in this book were written by Illinois poets, mostly from Joliet, who were commissioned to consider a sculpture, either at its site or from a photograph, and then to react either to the work itself, its subject, or its theme. Some of the poets were friends, acquaintances, or former students. Some responded to the advertisements online and in newspapers. The theory was to combine literary art with the visual arts of sculpture and photography.

I wasn't too surprised to find that some poets who had published their works in literary magazines or anthologies just couldn't write quality poems of this type. They were used to having no limitations of length or subject matter or deadlines, and they were not used to editors questioning their efforts. Consequently, they lost their commissions and other poets were found.

Most performed impressively and were appreciative of the editorial suggestions. They, like me, sometimes found themselves re-writing some of the poems over and over whereas others came almost instantly. I enjoyed meeting and working with them and many engaging people at the Friends of Community Public Art.

Nearly all of the poems are Free Verse, which means they don't follow metrical or rhyming patterns, though they may appeal to sound through rhythms of phrasing and repetitions of letters or words. Traditionally poems appeal to the sense of readers and their emotions more than to their brains or their powers of reasoning. Sometimes poems tell stories with characters and plots and dialogues. Other times they are more like essays or news reports with leads, sources, and evidence. They try to entertain, to instruct, to persuade, to inspire....

Carl Sandburg once wrote that poems are a "synthesis of biscuits and hyacinths." Hot or cool, tasting or fragrant, here are some Joliet poems inspired by the eye candy of photography and sculpture inspired, in turn, by the environs and history of the community.

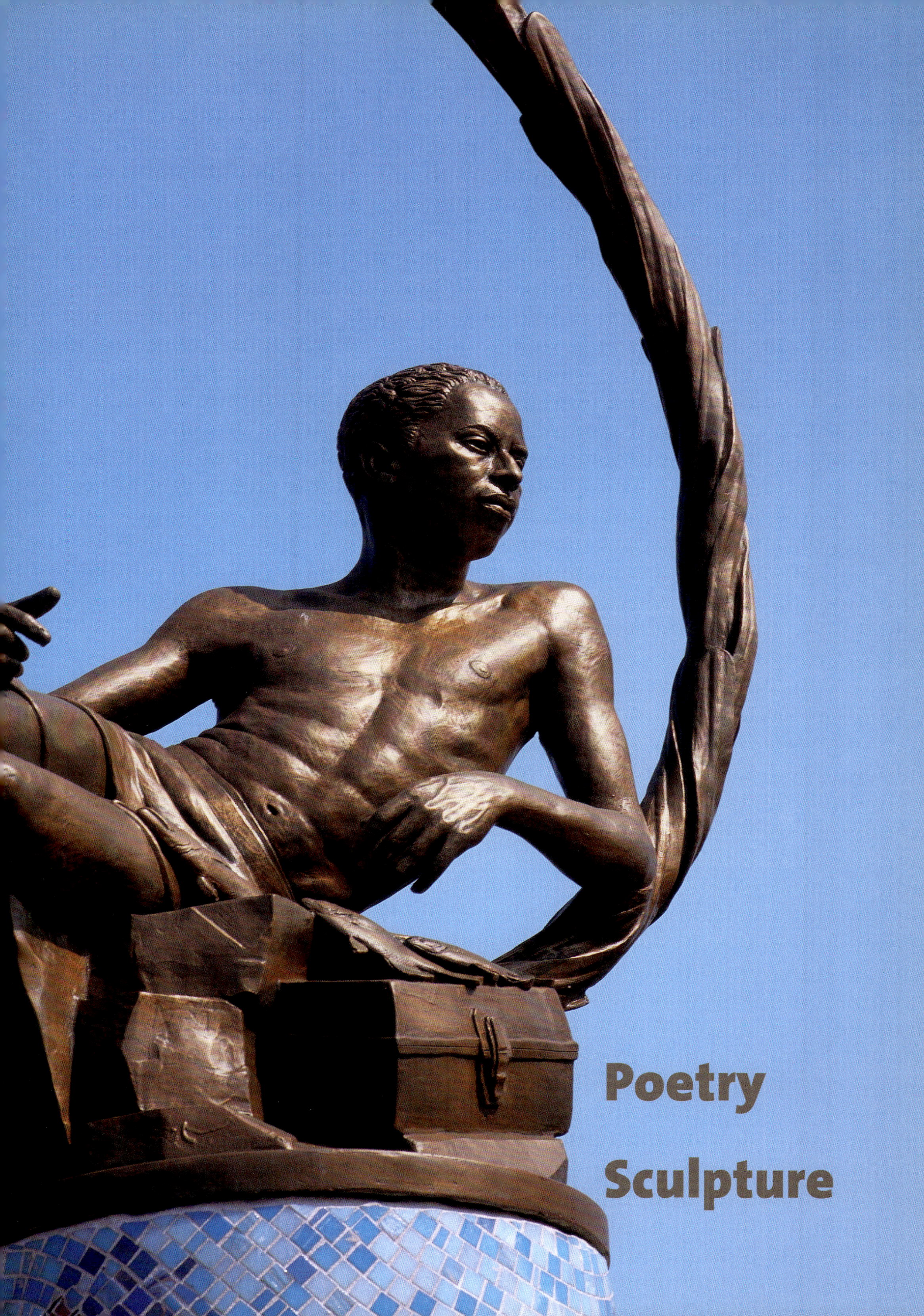
Poetry
Sculpture

1

Concrete Rivers

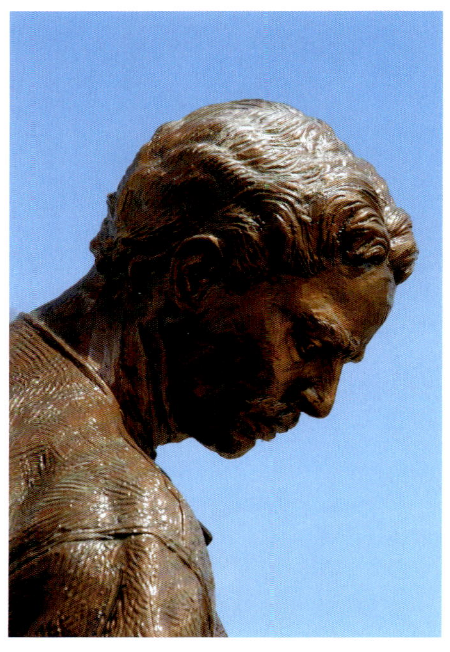

Roads are concrete rivers

We build 'em
People drive on 'em

Shovelfuls of shared chivalry

Filling in grids with asphalt
Is like playing tic-tac-toe

Patches of history
Tattooed on crust

Toes cramped into boots
Scream for release

Into a farce

More interesting
Than ebbs and flows

Trial and error
Traffic crusading

Fulminating
In the open air

GEORGE DAVID MILLER

history

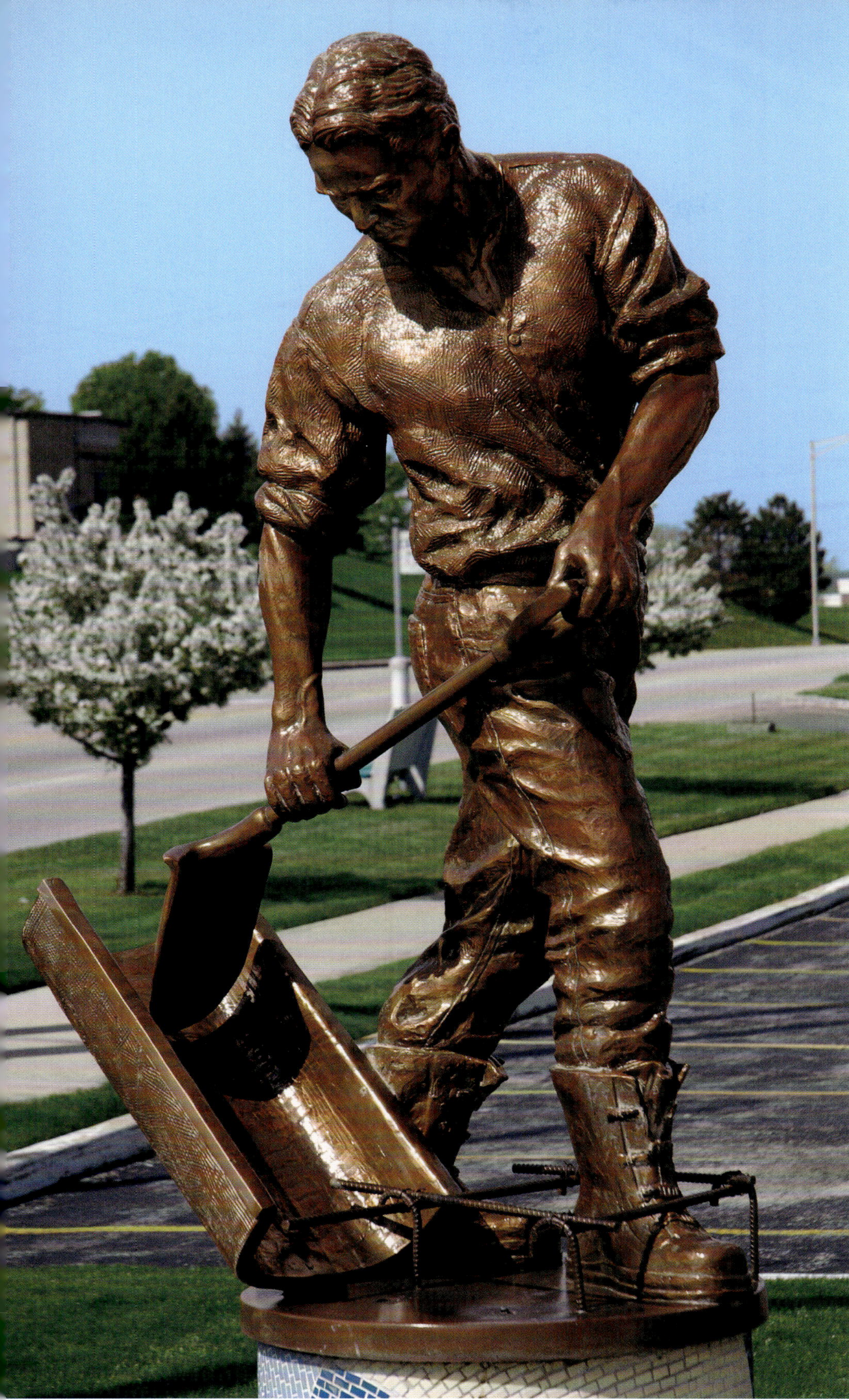

Building the Lincoln Highway

SCULPTURE

LEAD ARTIST
Kathleen Farrell

ASSISTANT ARTISTS
Dante DiBartolo,
Roberta Faulhaber,
Sharka Glet,
Emile Sauer

MOSAIC

LEAD ARTIST
David Yanchick

2

Route 66

Fenders and bridges,
Motels and diners,
Alpha of Chicago to
Santa Monica's Omega—
A monument to a dream.

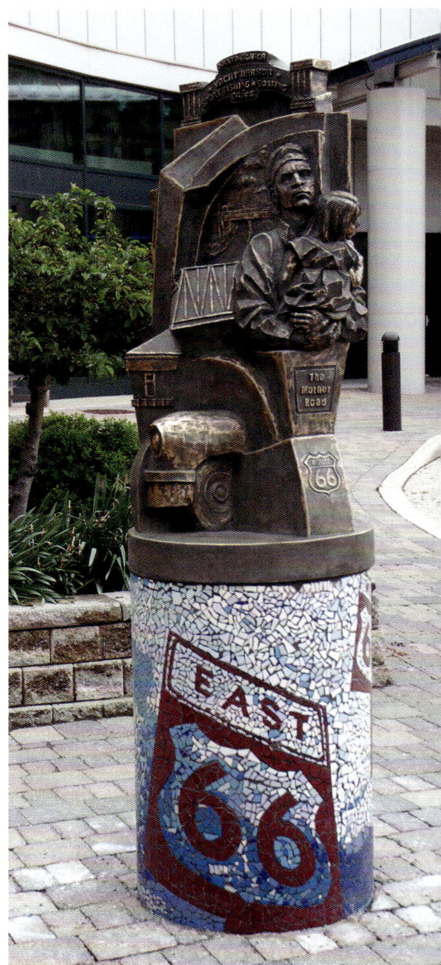

"To a road," you say?
Nostalgia for old asphalt?
No, not the road
But what it promised.
The last of a century of pioneers
Traveled that road in beat-up Chevies,
Getting their kicks dreaming of new beginnings
Until the west filled up
Into megalopolis,
And the dream faded
Into the smog and gridlock
Of an outsourced reality.

But while the dream motored on
America was young
And believed it could do anything—
And that anything it did was right.
Now we enshrine that road—
Writing elegies to our lost innocence,
Erecting this tombstone for the dream.

TED THOMPSON

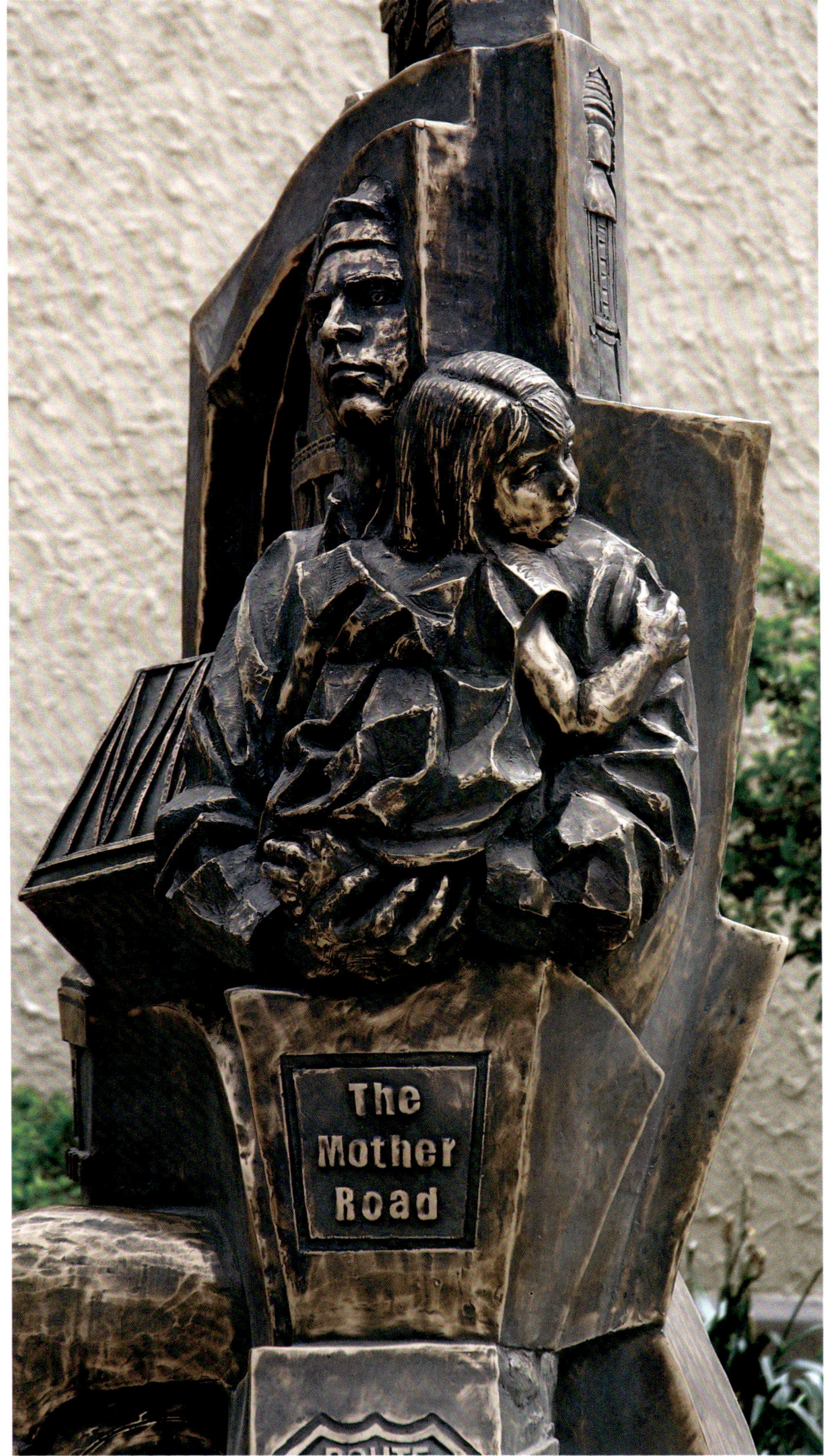

Route 66:
The Mother Road

SCULPTURE

LEAD ARTIST
Kathleen Scarboro

ASSISTANT ARTIST
David Yanchick

MOSAIC

LEAD ARTIST
Sharka Glet

ASSISTANT ARTIST
Shane Jackson

Veteran Women: Proudly They Serve

SCULPTURE

LEAD ARTIST
Jesus Rodriguez

MOSAIC

LEAD ARTIST
Dante DiBartolo

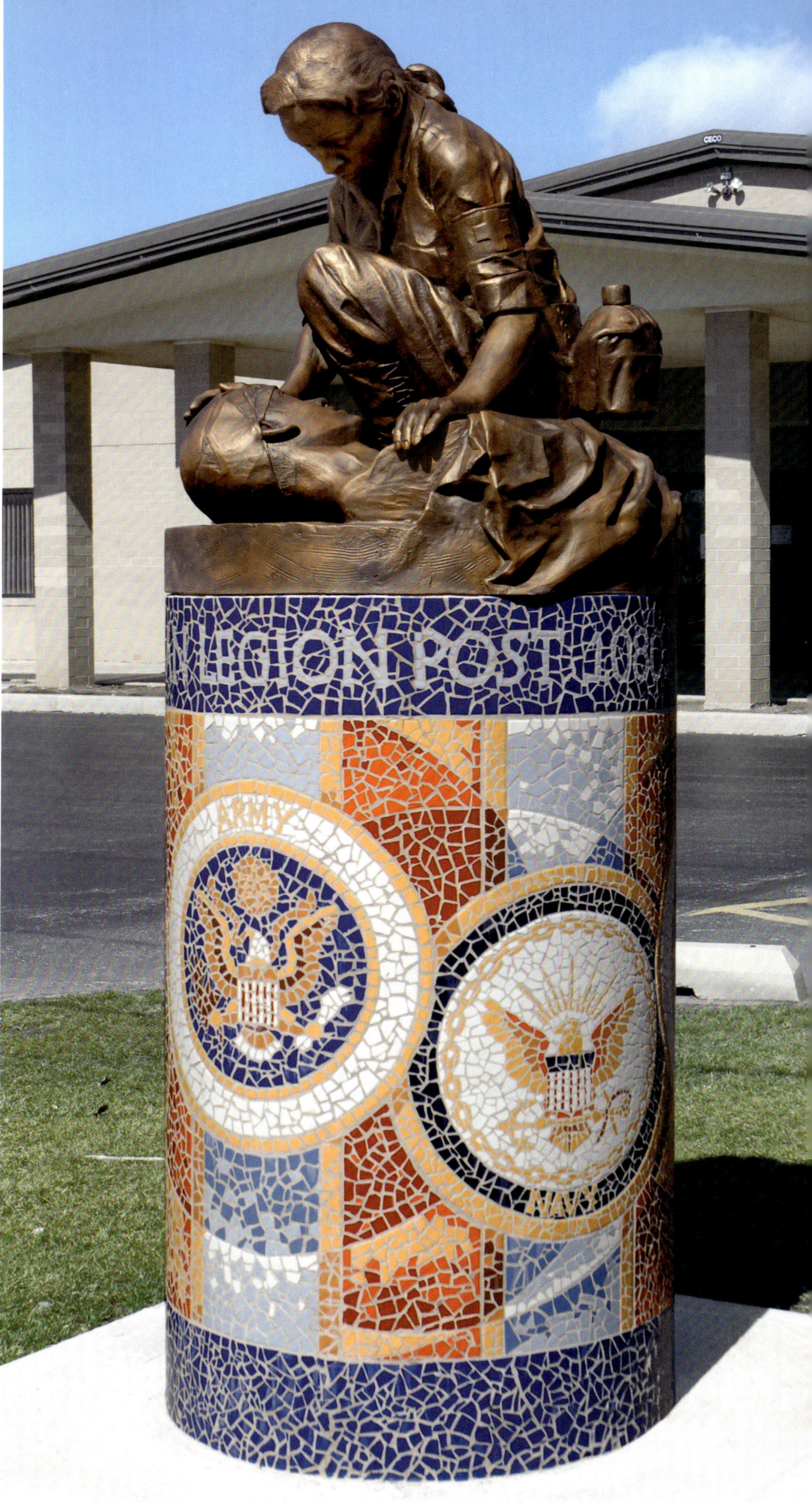

Joliet's Female Veterans

Long before Sally Ride skyed into space
Or Amelia Earheart, aviatrix, disappeared in the Pacific,
American women have been headliners for heroics.
Remember Pocahontas saving John Smith at Jamestown
Or Anne Hutchinson leading her congregation from Massachusetts.
Consider Sacagawea's exploits with Lewis and Clark out West.
These women are legendary for their courage and skill.
The legends continued with Molly Pitcher at BunkerHill
Then Barbara Frietchie at Fredericksburg.
As the glamour of warfare was dulled by cannons
And bombardments of nitro and T.N.T.
First Florence Nightingale in England then Clara Barton in America
Organized Orders of the Red Cross to minister to the wounded.
In W.W.I the American novelist Edith Wharton
Continued their work near the trenches in France.
Joliet's female corpsman looks military and tough
But her courage is booted and laced with tenderness
She risks injury and death to kill pain and fear
On the battlefield or in the theater of war.
Joliet Wacs, Waves, or Wafs, during and since W.W.II
Have made us realize that flying, shooting, or bombing
Are not the only Special Forces at War.

JOHN STOBART

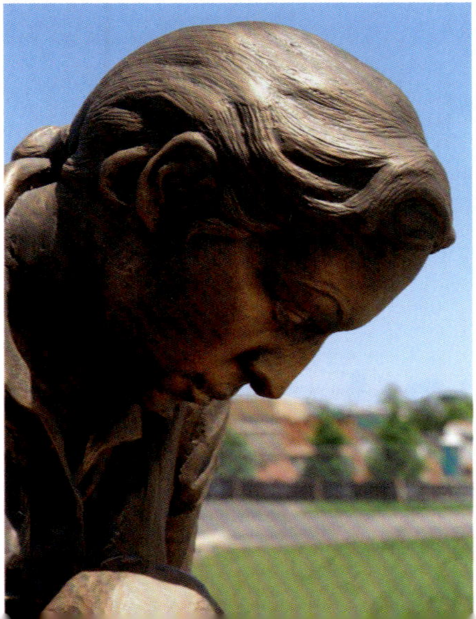

Sandy Sanchez

He was a shield
Between light and dark
A rapier taunting
Encroaching strife.

Courage courts Death
And eventually
Death accepts
The proposal.

Underneath
Collective sighs
Of relief
Belief sings
In perfect pitch.

Mission
Accomplished
Mission
Complete
He stands in the shadows
We dance in the streets.

GEORGE DAVID MILLER

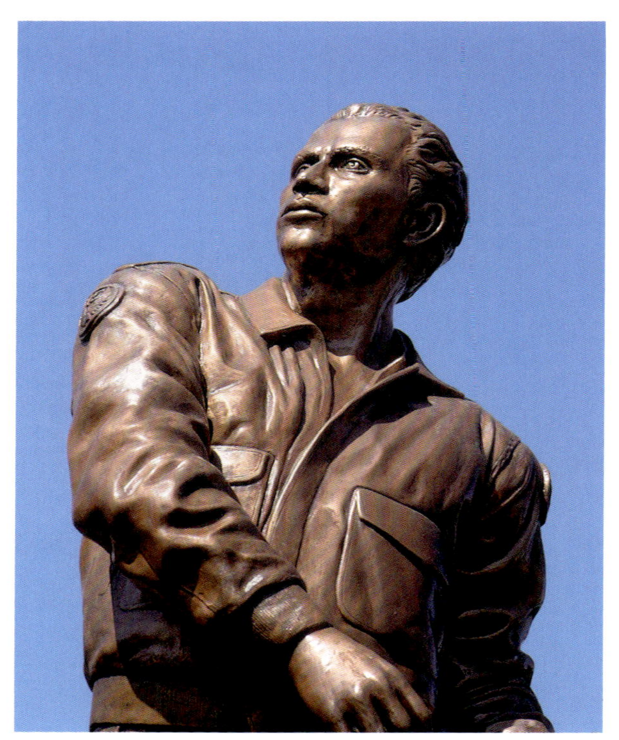

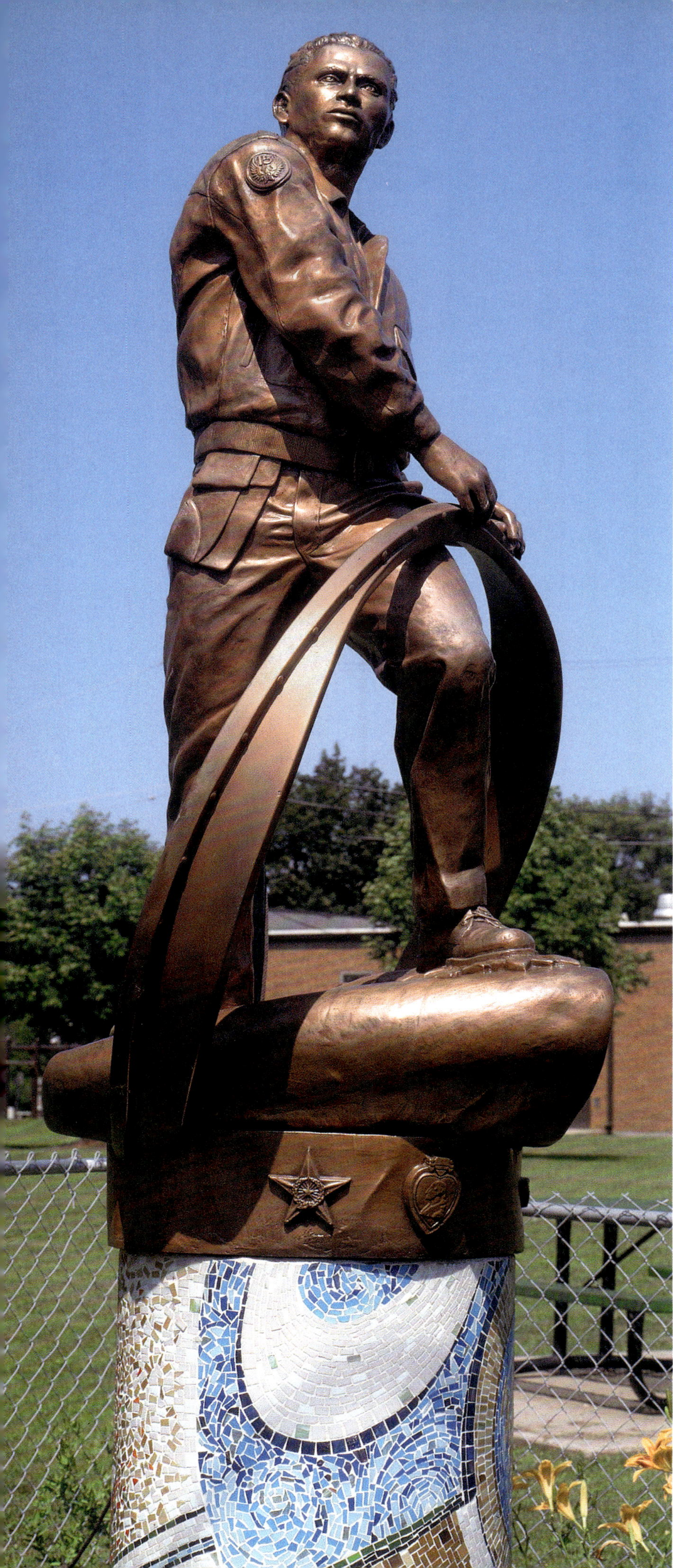

Sator Sanchez: World War II Hero

SCULPTURE

LEAD ARTIST
Kathleen Farrell

LEAD ASSISTANT ARTIST
Dante DiBartolo, Andrea Rountree

ASSISTANT ARTISTS
Saul Chavira, Roger Carlson

MOSAIC

LEAD ARTIST
Ilario Silva

The Story of Sator "Sandy" Sanchez

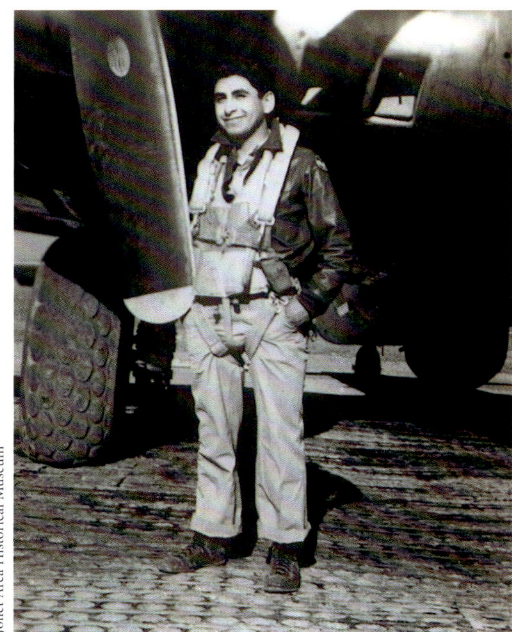
Joliet Area Historical Museum

Sator "Sandy" Sanchez was born on March 22, 1921, and grew up in the Hispanic community in Joliet, Illinois. His early years were an ordeal; while he was only 2 years old, Sanchez's mother died from tuberculosis and later, when he was 8 his father was murdered. Adopted by his grandparents, Sanchez dreamed of flying airplanes. Often, he rode his bicycle to Lewis airport to watch the planes come and go. While attending Joliet Township High School, he joined a junior reserve officer training corps unit. And after graduation, Sanchez worked for the Civilian Conservation Corps.

In 1939, he joined the Army and became an aircraft mechanic in 1941. After the outbreak of War World II, in 1943, he began his combat career with the 8TH Air Force, 95TH Bomb Group, 334TH Bombardment Squadron as a tail gunner in a Boeing B-17 "Flying Fortress" bomber. On Oct. 10, 1943, during a mission over Munster, Germany, Sanchez shot down two enemy aircrafts, a Messerschmitt ME-109 and a Junkers JU-88. For this mission, he was awarded a Silver Star.

Only twenty-five missions were required per service tour, but Sanchez volunteered to stay and completed forty-four missions before he took his leave. In recognition of his dedication, a B-17 was named for him, the "Smilin' Sandy Sanchez," the only known case of a B-17 having been named for an enlisted man. After six months in the United States, the 23-year-old Sanchez volunteered for what would be his third combat tour. He was sent to the 15TH Air Force in Lucera, Italy, and was assigned to the 353RD Bomb Squadron, 301ST Bomb Group.

Sanchez died on March 15, 1945, during a mission to bomb an oil plant in Ruhland, Germany, manning the top gun turret position. While attempting to bomb the oil plant, the B-17 was hit by flak and severely damaged. As the crew members bailed out, Sanchez stayed with the aircraft, manning his gun. The aircraft exploded and broke into several pieces. The Germans, who captured the nine surviving crewmembers that had jumped, told pilot Dale Thornton that they had buried Sanchez next to the B-17. However, Sanchez's body was never recovered, and six weeks later the war in Europe ended.

Sator "Sandy" Sanchez was one of the most highly decorated U.S. Army Air Forces enlisted crew members. Sanchez's medals included the Silver Star for Bravery in Action, Soldier's Medal for Bravery for jumping into a runaway plane and stopping it before it hit a hanger that contained other planes and crewmen, Distinguished Flying Cross for Bravery While in Flight, Air Medal with Eight Oak Leaf Clusters, and the Purple Heart for being wounded in action. Sanchez was posthumously awarded the ninth and tenth Oak Leaf Clusters and a second Purple Heart.

The Story of Katherine Dunham

Katherine Dunham's life of bridging cultures together began through an early exposure to and love of dance. Artist and humanitarian, Katherine Dunham was born in Chicago, Illinois, in 1909 of African-American, French-Canadian, and Native American ancestry. When she was 5 years old, Dunham's family moved to Joliet, Illinois, where her father opened a dry-cleaning shop. An exceptional athlete, Dunham first studied dance at Joliet Township High School and Joliet Junior College. She moved to Chicago in 1927 and studied tap-dancing, ballet, and acting. In the early 1930s, she opened a dance school and performed at the Chicago Opera House and the Chicago World's Fair. In 1935, while on scholarship at the University of Chicago, she won the prestigious Rosenwald Foundation Travel Fellowship and took her first field trip to the West Indies to study Afro-Caribbean dance, religion, and folklore. A year later she received a Bachelor's of Art degree in anthropology from the University of Chicago.

The West Indian experience forever changed the focus of Dunham's life. This initial fieldwork in 1935 began her lifelong involvement with the people and dance of Haiti. From this experience Dunham composed her master thesis (the University of Chicago, 1947) and wrote three books about her observations: *Journey to Accompong* (1946), *The Dances of Haiti* (her master thesis, published in 1947), and *Island Possessed* (1969).

Dunham developed her unique combination of traditional ballet and African dance forms as dance director of the Works Progress Administration's Federal Theatre Project in Chicago. In the late 1930s, her troupe performed in New York, Chicago, and at various places in Illinois, including a high school scholarship benefit in Joliet. She also choreographed dance scenes for Warner Brothers' movies, and lectured and wrote on anthropological subjects. In 1939, Katherine married Canadian-born, John Pratt, a painter and costume and set designer.

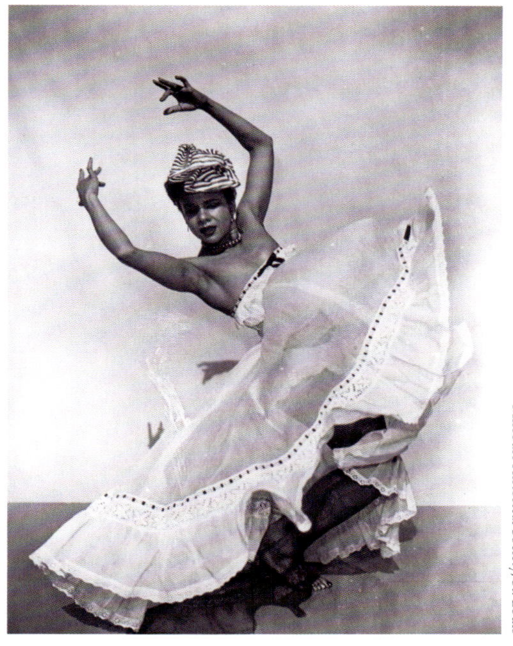

Missouri Historical Society, St. Louis

In 1940, Dunham's all-black musical drama *Cabin in the Sky* was staged on Broadway and in San Francisco. In 1943, she appeared in the black movie classic *Stormy Weather* with Lena Horne, Fats Waller, and Cab Calloway. Dunham opened the Katherine Dunham School of Dance in New York in 1944, which remained in existence for a decade. Over the next sixteen years, the Katherine Dunham Dancers appeared in films, plays, and television specials, and they recorded albums while also touring to rave reviews in Mexico, Latin America, Western Europe, the Near and Far East, and Australia and New Zealand.

In 1967, Dunham moved to East St. Louis, Illinois, where she has been affiliated with Southern Illinois University. She founded the East St. Louis Center for the Performing Arts, the Katherine Dunham Children's Workshop, and a museum that hold items from her troupe and its travels. She has received numerous awards and maintained an active interest in civil rights and international affairs until her death on May 21, 2006.

Madame Dunham

Rhythm of Haiti in your hips, you transcended the
Vaudeville of your time and transformed from ballerina
into Congo beats pulsating through hallways of academia.
Voodoo priestess and doctor of Cultural Anthropology,
Groundbreaking spirit so overflowing with femininity.
East St. Louis loves you. Carbondale embraces you.
University of sweet home Chicago, endlessly sends praises too.
"Est-il femme plus provoquatrice que vous?
Une femme plus creatrice et juste?"
I think not, madame, as you have invoked Loa directly,
Matriarch of black dance and unprecedented lady.
"I used to want the words 'She tried' on my tombstone."
–Katherine Dunham

KATHERINNE BARDALES

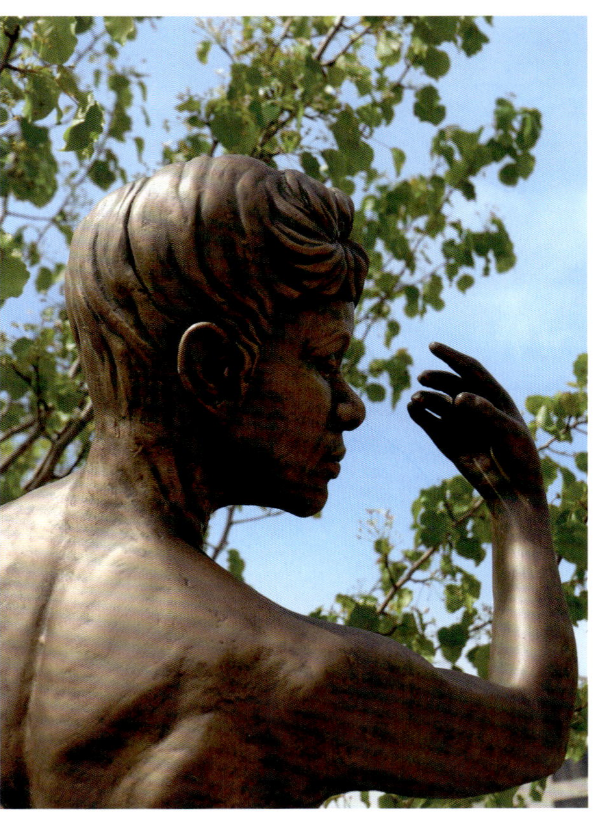

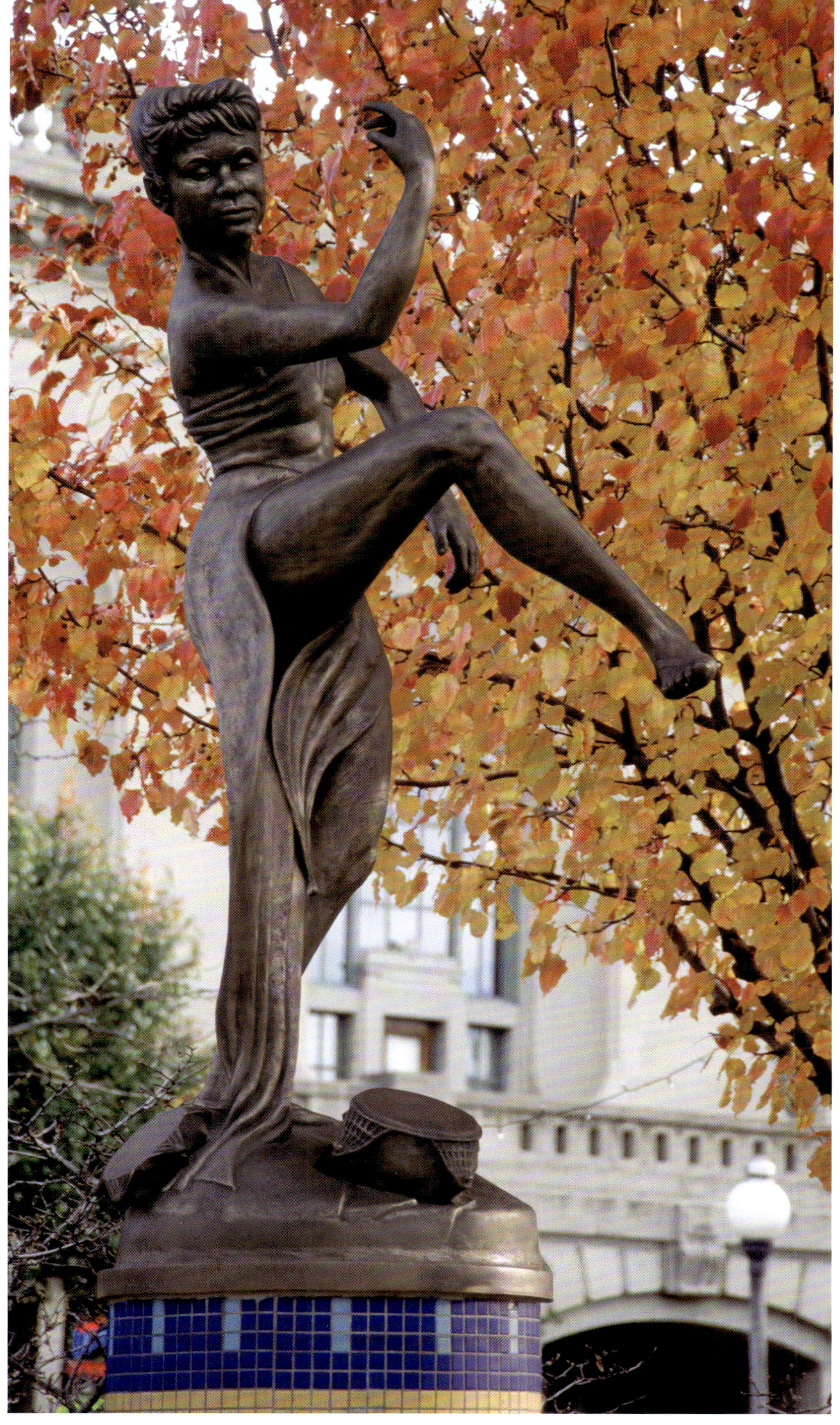

Katherine Dunham: Dancer, Choreographer and Citizen

SCULPTURE

LEAD ARTIST
Kathleen Farrell

ASSISTANT ARTISTS
Sarah Furst, Dante DiBartolo, Roger Carlson

MOSAIC

SIMPLE MOSAIC

Goaltender

At 6'10", George Mikan was the first dominant big man in professional basketball and its first true superstar.

What I like
to remember
are the guys
who said height
was a handicap,
freakish. Jokes
about my shorts
size and what size
underneath. Guys
who wouldn't look
me in the eye, laughed
at my feet, thumbs,
parts they envied.
But balls good
as grounded
when I tended goal
and later they made
it illegal, what I did
and how I did it.
Then I surprised
them with my
speed. Once
scored 53 points
against the entire
team of Rhode
Island State.
For years,
what I liked
best of all: to rise
up, swat away each tiny
planet like so many words
scattering under my hands.

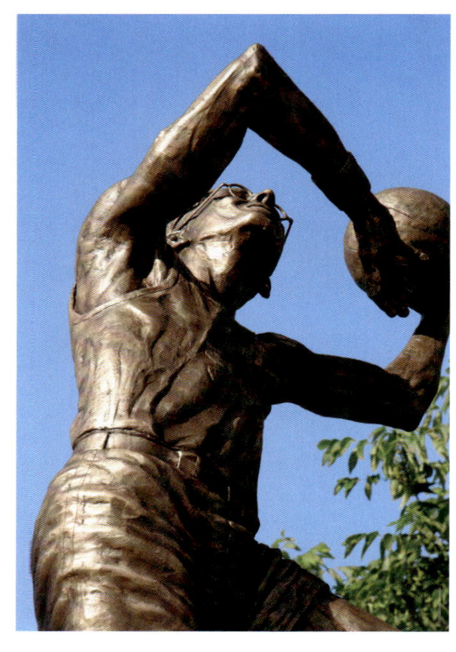

VALERIA MARTTS WALLACE

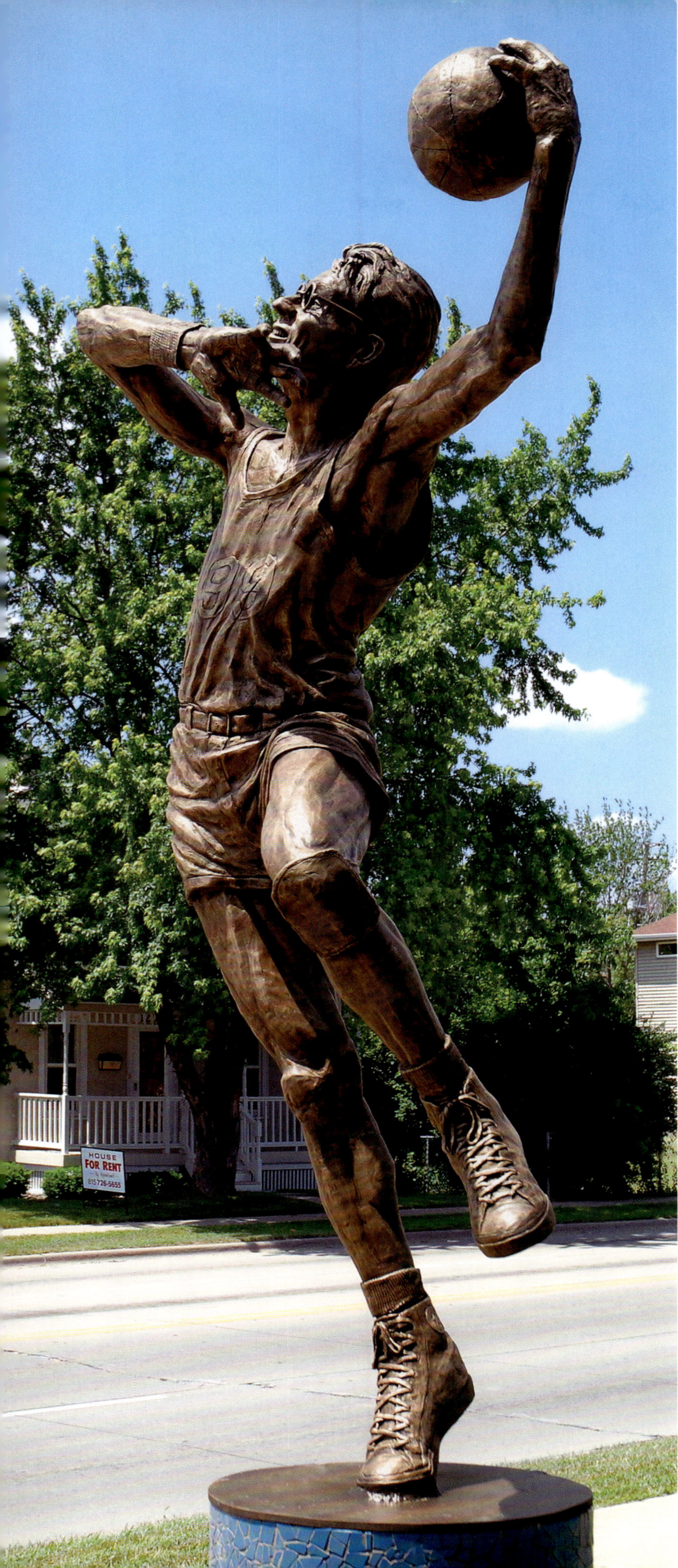

George Mikan: Changed the Game of Basketball Forever

SCULPTURE

LEAD ARTIST
David Standifer

ASSISTANT ARTIST
Dante DiBartolo

MOSAIC

SIMPLE MOSAIC

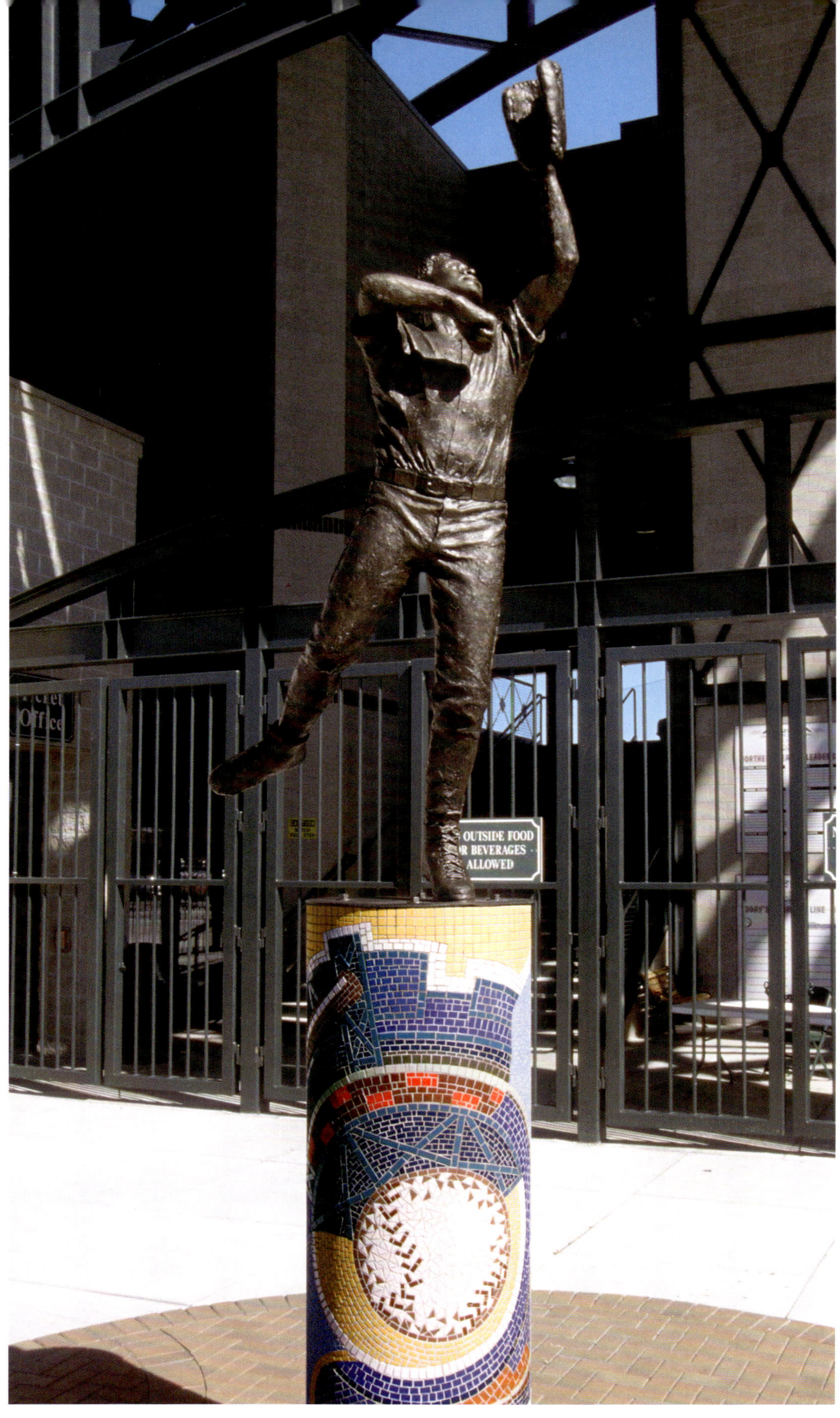

Jesse Barfield: A Great Joliet Baseball Tradition

SCULPTURE		MOSAIC
LEAD ARTIST	ASSISTANT LEAD ARTIST	LEAD ARTIST
Kathleen Farrell	**Sharka Glet, Dante DiBartolo, Annick Bailly**	**Saul Chavira**

7

Joliet's Jesse

The chant for young Jesse was "Knock, Knock, Knock!"
Cause he belted the long ball from Belmont Park.
Then he danced round center field for the Steelmen of J.T.
And dueled with J.C.'s Gullicksen to make his mark.
The scouts from the bigs come for Gully's killer k's
But Jesse zoned and zonked two over the tower
And chased down balls to the walls with grace and power.
Joliet saw a future great from their town
Major League Golden Gloves and a Homerun Crown.
Master of the swing; artist of the catch
Joliet and Jesse Barfield, a forever match.

STEVE BROADWAY

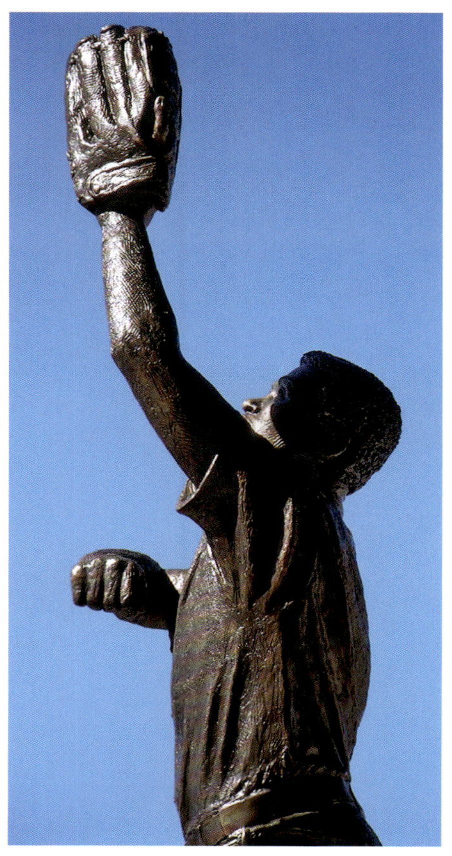

A Policeman is the Semaphore of Civilization

There's no virtue in anonymity,
in isolation, in stoicism, in silence.
There's no happiness in loneliness,
oscillation, persecution, fear.
There's no resurrection in resentment,
hatred, indifference, pride.
There's no rescue in the selfish dark.

We are the deed's creature
We are creatures
We are of the flowers
We are De Flores

There's no one alive who wouldn't
undo the past, no one in our past
who wouldn't rejoice to hold us again,
no hold we can grip to help us climb
the fog. We're alone and besieged
by badness. We crave rescue, but
there's only rescue in the selfless dark.

We are creatures
We are the deed's creature
We are De Flores
We are of the flowers

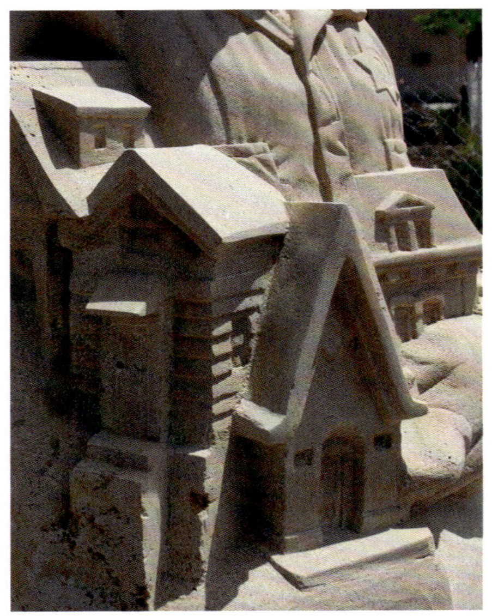

WILLIAM PAUL YARROW

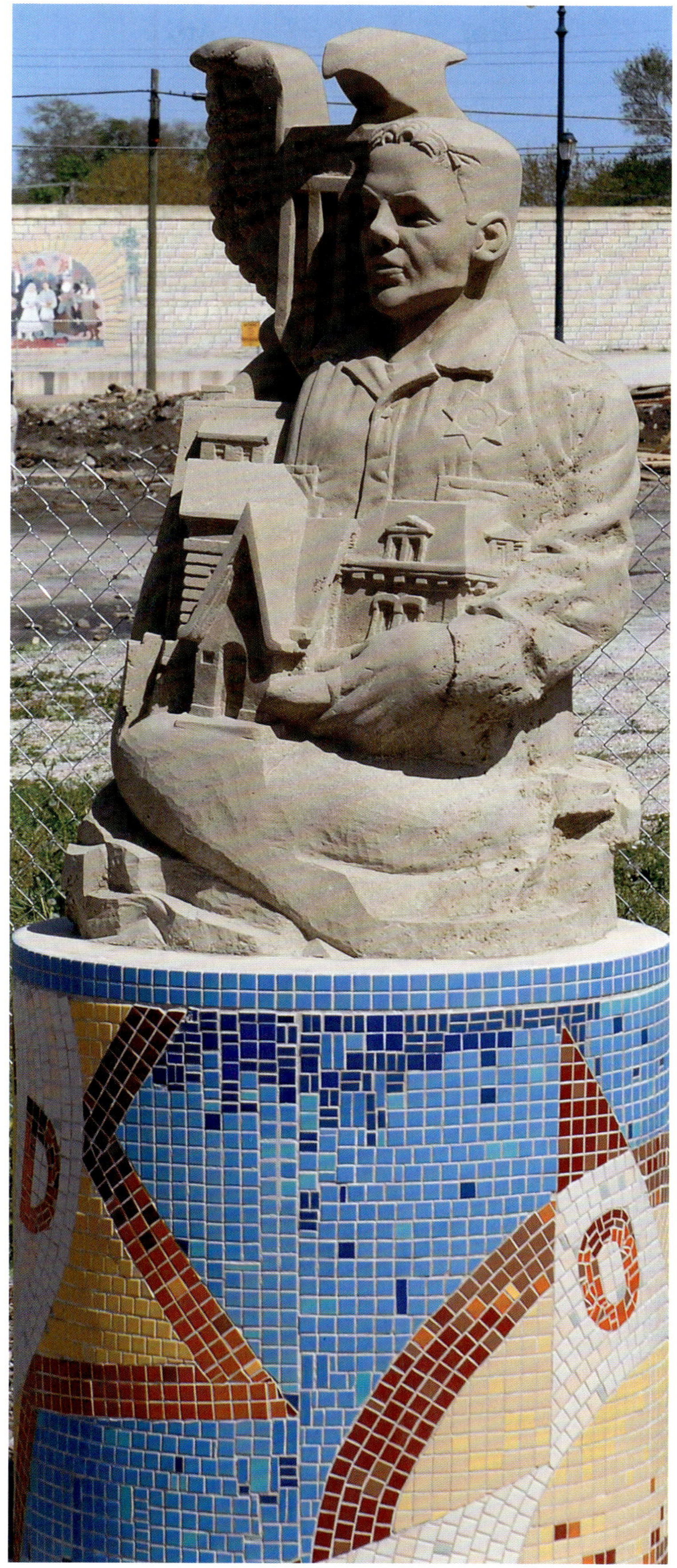

Community Policing: Working with Citizens for a Safer City

SCULPTURE

LEAD ARTIST
Jesus Rodriguez

MOSAIC

LEAD ARTIST
Jesus Rodriguez

Joliet Fire Fighters: Helping Hands, Caring Hearts

SCULPTURE

LEAD ARTIST
Kathleen Farrell

LEAD ASSISTANT ARTIST
Sharka Glet, Dante DiBartolo

MOSAIC

LEAD ARTIST
Kathleen Farrell

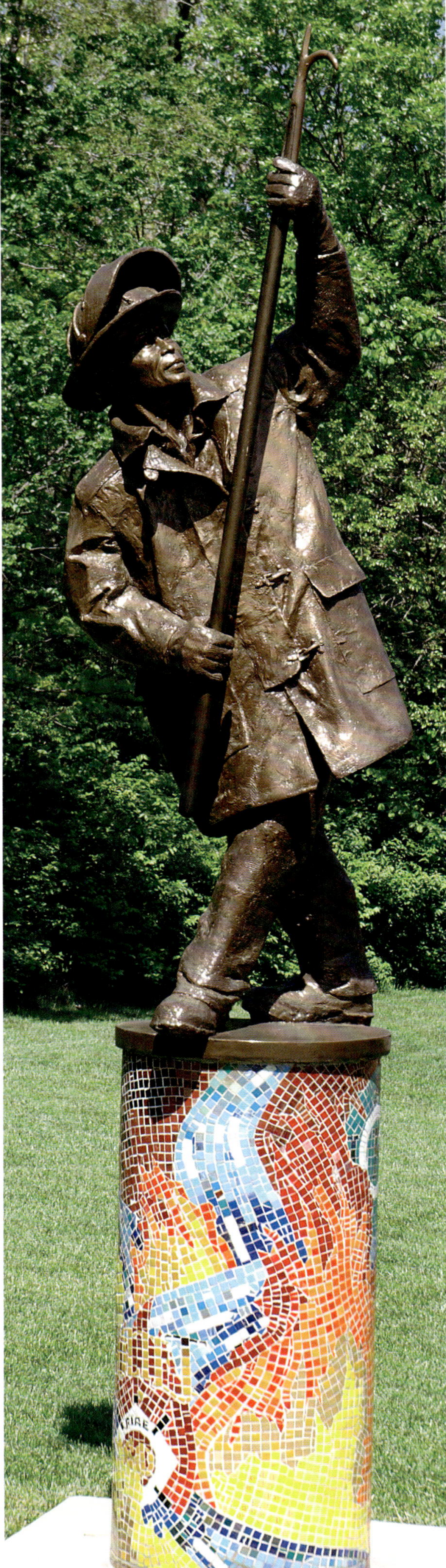

Firefighter

under the weight
of sooty boots
dregs of
beds, dressers, tables, and chairs
crumble.

a grappling hook
spears a chunk
of charred wood
once a windowsill.

after a fire
there is
residual heat
smoke in eyes
scents of sadness
diffusion of attention
debris of dreams.

GEORGE DAVID MILLER

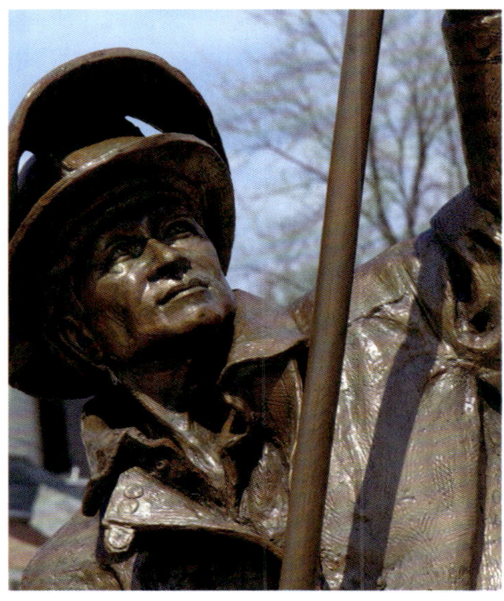

The Bison's Alimony

The bison know a lot about Longfellow
and wisteria and patrimony, the piscine nuance
of the clouds, God's topological integument.
They understand the orphan arroyo; they intuit
the numinous prairie. They predict a wooly
suburbia. Bison powerwalk my imagination.
I smell, in their arrayed dreaming, the sedimentary,
austere inference, traces of deciduous magnetism.
Under the nettled knot of august sunshine,
in the shadow of the reddened face of the future,
alongside the maternal mystery of the unused river,
the bison make their summary judgments, exact
retribution from the enacted masters of wistfulness,
and pay somber alimony to the ghost of an ochre wife.

WILLIAM PAUL YARROW

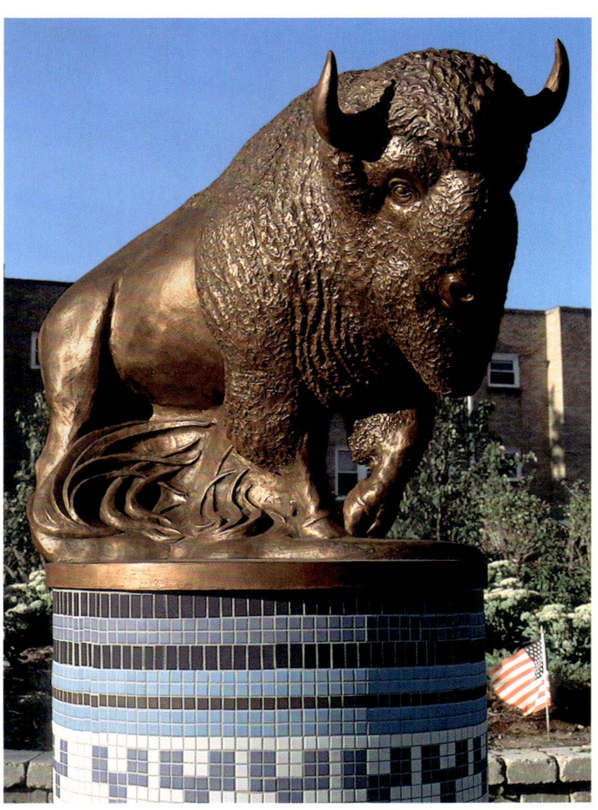

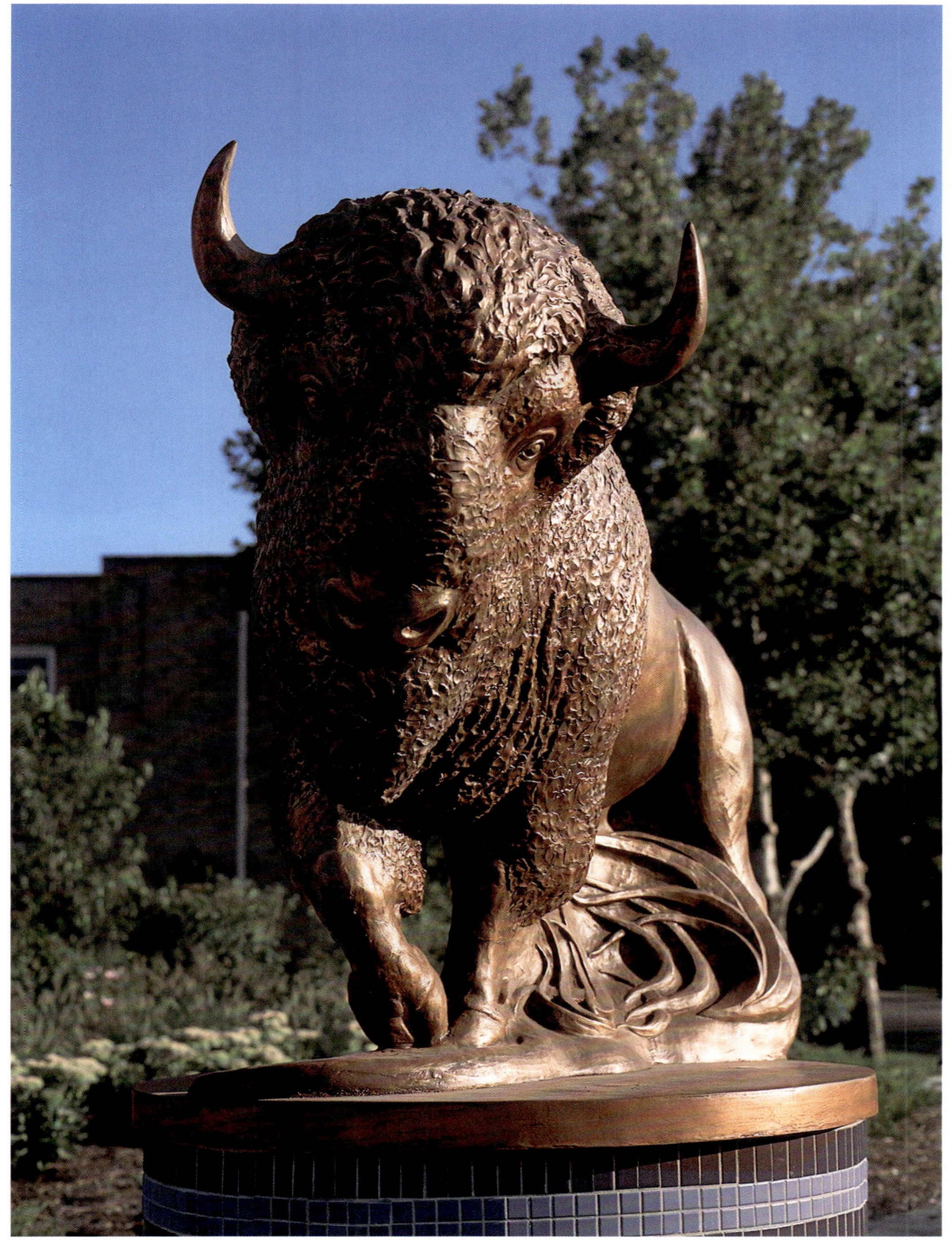

Monarch of the Prairie

SCULPTURE

LEAD ARTIST
Sarah Furst

ASSISTANT ARTISTS
Dante DiBartolo

MOSAIC

SIMPLE MOSAIC

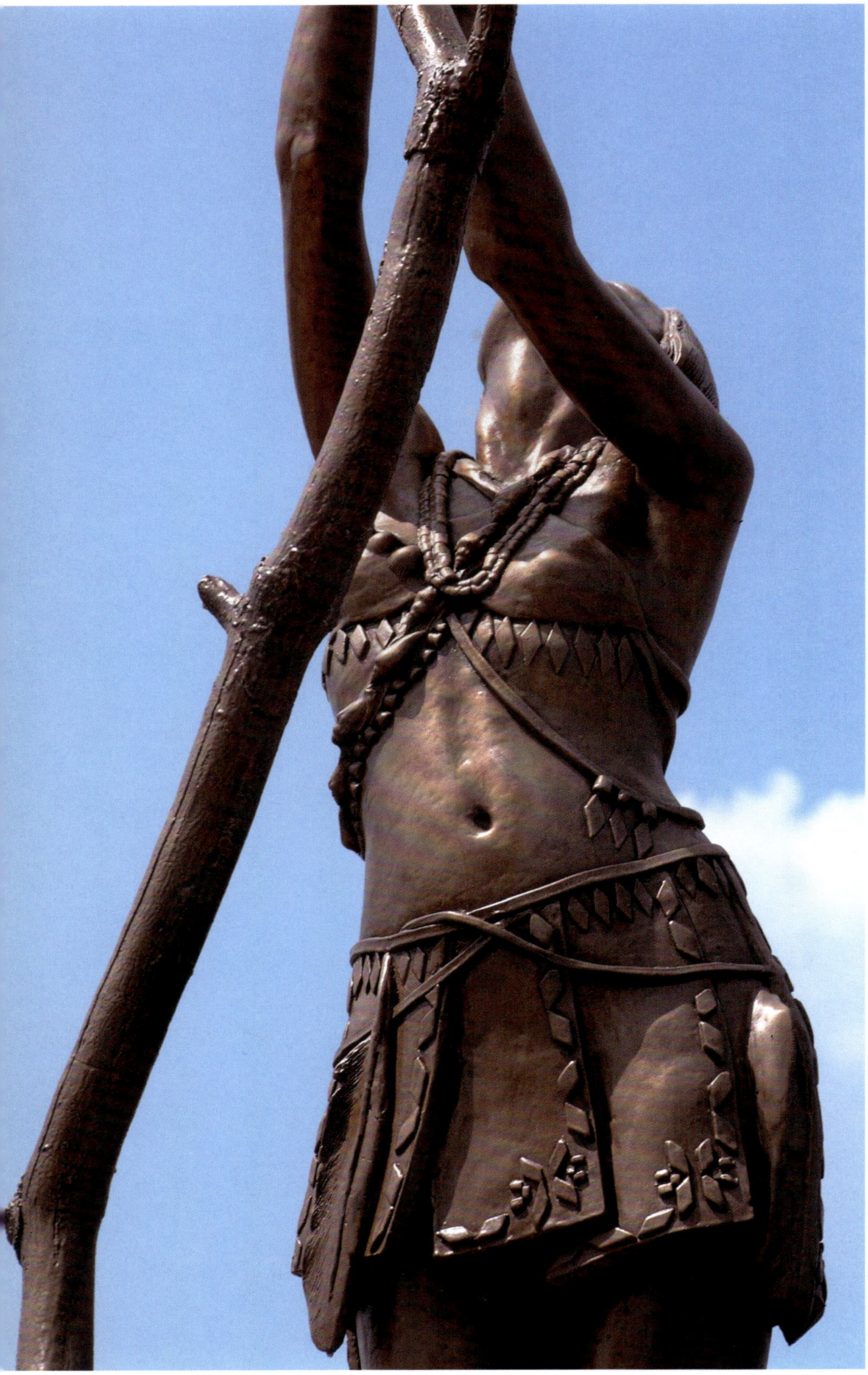

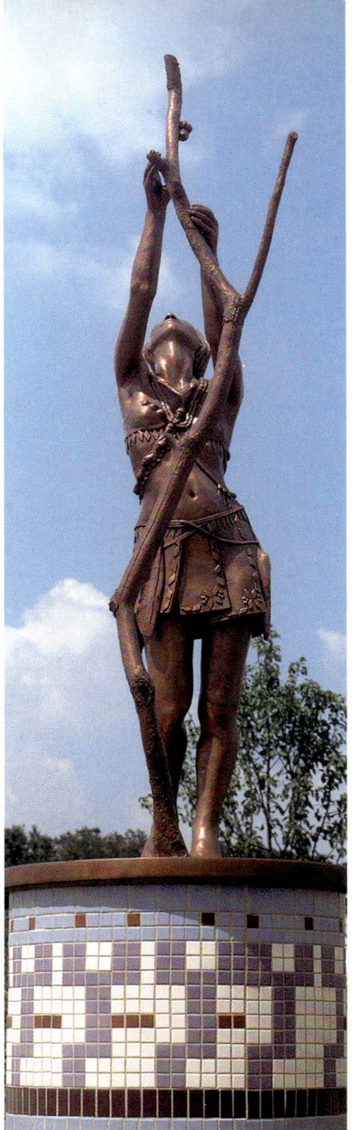

Asakiwaki Woman

SCULPTURE

LEAD ARTIST
Kathleen Scarboro

MOSAIC

SIMPLE MOSAIC

They Endured

This nubile Asakiwaki spoke Algonquin
And lived in wigwams, as did the Fox,
Ojibway, Blackfeet, and many other tribes.
She represents a centuries-old migrant culture,
Traveling South-West in early spring to cultivated land
With reliable rainfall and growing seasons
Then North-East to hunt and gather woodland's nuts and berries.
SNOWBIRDS

Their lives were complicated and enriched by French explorers
And missionaries, traders and trappers
Who gave them beads and crosses, sold them guns and whiskey
And frequently impregnated them.
At first they were friendly to the English too,
But the "blue eyes" built farms on their fields
And forbade them their traditional hunting camps and streams
Chief Blackhawk resisted but lost the war.
SNOWBIRDS NO LONGER

Algonquins migrated West, following the buffalo
But were hounded by the Union Pacific
Which demolished all obstacles in its path
Especially the buffalo but also mountains and tribes.
Algonquins were herded on reservations for generations.

Today, Asakiwaki are known to few.
But this maiden's descendents still might be seen
Jingle dancing at Joliet Jr. College's Annual Powow
Or playing with children's dream catchers
At Romeoville's Lily Cache Museum.

JOHN STOBART

Progressive Pioneer

It was an African American known only
as Bob who first saw this area's potential
as a crossroads of commerce
and intercultural cooperation.

The rivers and paths through the woods,
wetlands and prairies—as now, more fully
paved—brought people of many backgrounds
and needs that cried out to be met.

Black, white, red,
skin color or culture didn't matter to Bob
back in the eighteenth century, when a fair
trade for all concerned was at stake.

As self-appointed intermediary, an entrepreneur
who lived among the Potowatomi and knew
close-up the ways of the European whites,
he had the forward-looking vision that would

serve all special interests then—and would
serve them now as well, if he were still
with us in more than sculptured memory.
His look and gait suggest an activism

sorely needed in his surroundings—where
even the loose-fitting shirt he wore was worth
a number of fur pelts in mosquito season—
and sorely needed now.

EARL VALENTINE FISCHER

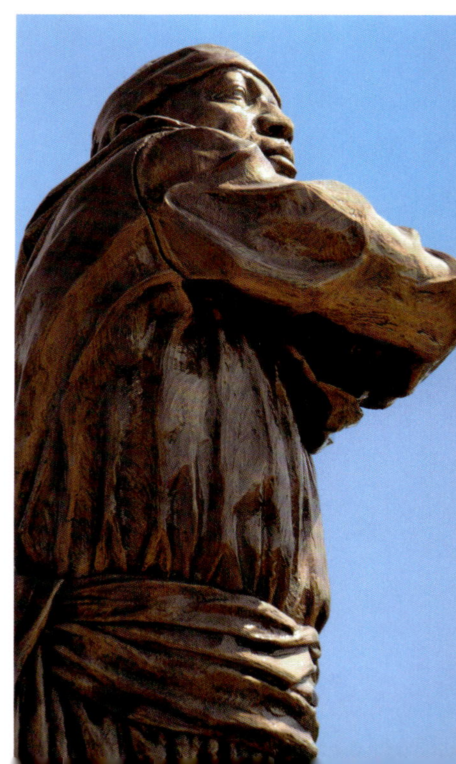

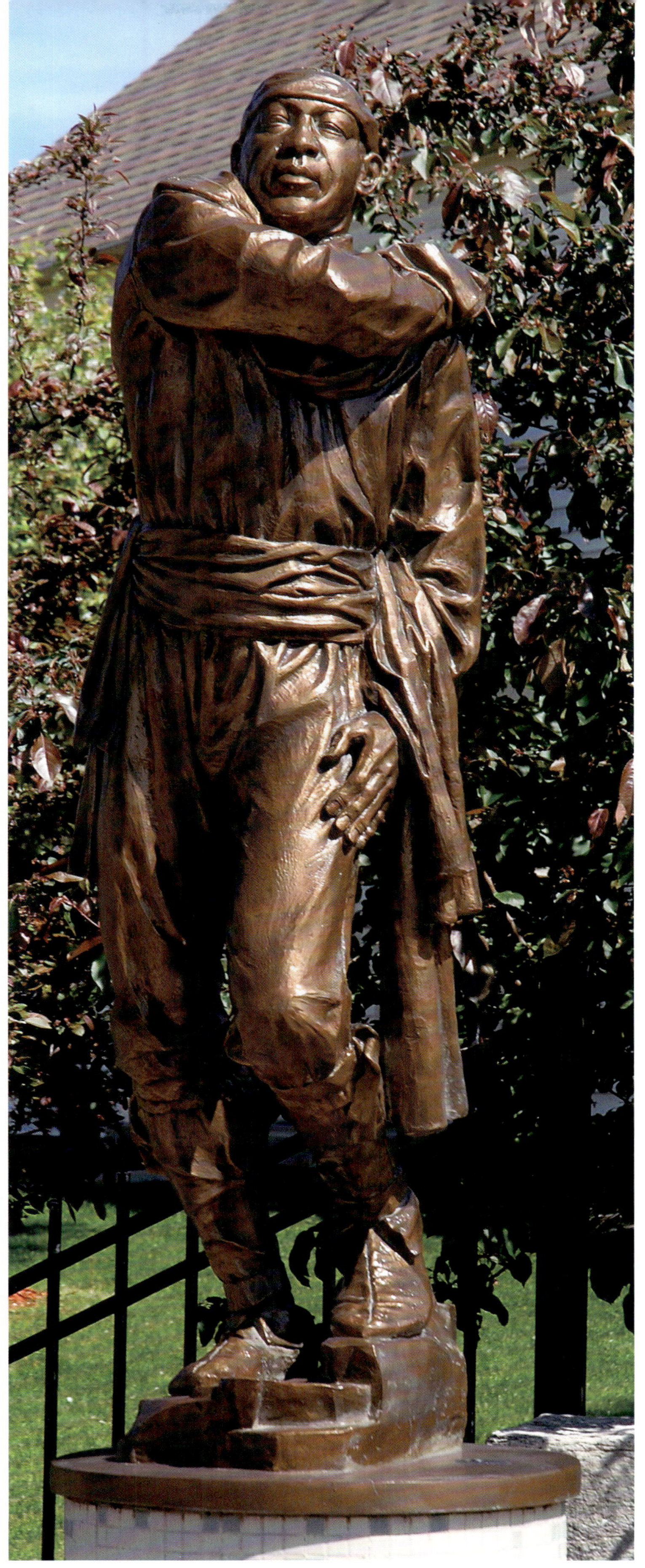

The First Pioneer

SCULPTURE

LEAD ARTIST
Jesus Rodriguez

MOSAIC

LEAD ARTIST
Jesus Rodriguez

1850s Barber: Underground Railroad Hero

SCULPTURE

LEAD ARTIST
Kathleen Farrell

ASSISTANT ARTISTS
Dante DiBartolo, Sarah Furst, Saul Chavira

MOSAIC

LEAD ARTIST
Kreshaun McKinney

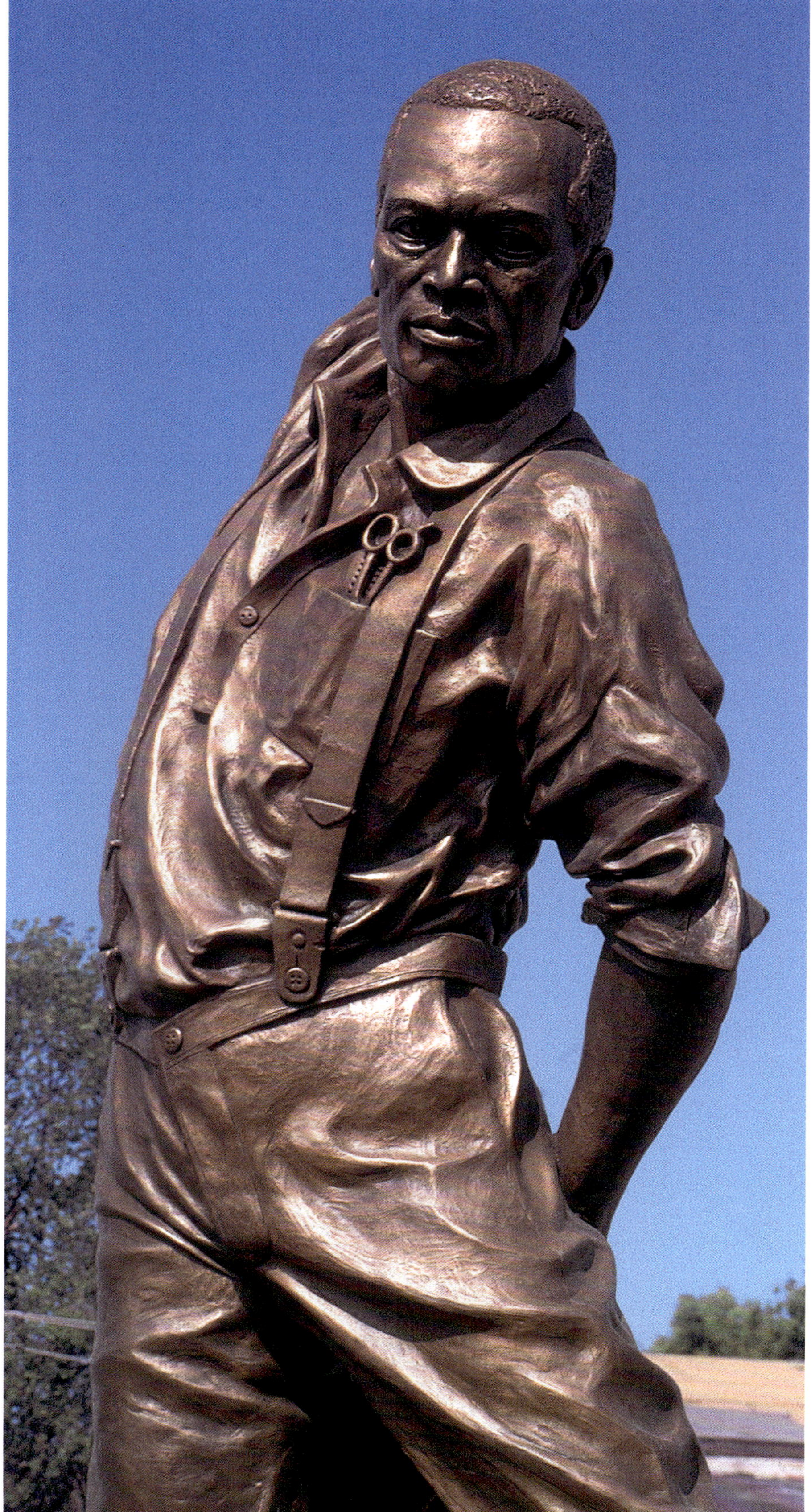

Together From the Start

When the land of Will was newly born,
White men held all the bounty:
They crushed the innocent, forfeited and scorned;
This history shaped our county.

One man seems like a myth in a maze
Though it's clear how he spent the century.
He traveled, he settled, he took up a trade.
It seemed he was where he ought to be.

Yet, this black barber was hunted like game,
Not a drop of hope to slake his thirst.
One judge upheld the "Fugitive" claim
While two bounty hunters schemed to get him first.

But Henry's friends tried another route
One man's shop had a floor that rose
It concealed Henry safe, caused no doubt
This friend, though white, our hero chose.

Henry came west from Pennsylvania, already free
Here, though, he hid, bent over like a tree;
Whispering wind, invisibly,
His lion heart continues in memory.

KIM VOLLMER-LAWSON

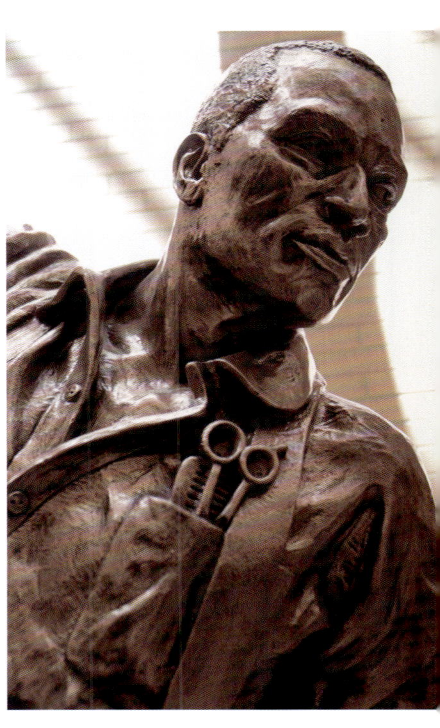

14

Founding Father

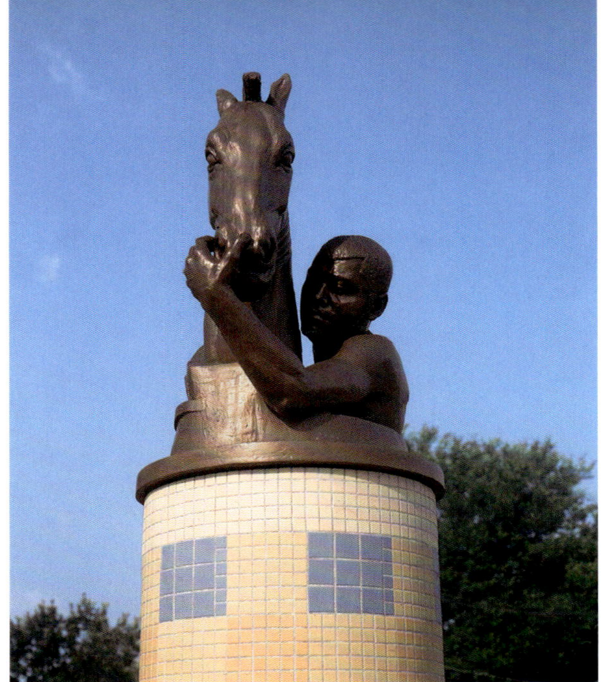

The horse had no blinders;
The man, however,
Saw neither right nor left
And ahead only as far
As sundown.
To his way of thinking,
No pioneer, he,
Just a prairie farmer
Planting a crop,
Feeding a family,
Paying the bank loan,
Knowing only necessity,
Today's mud and manure,
Dreaming only of harvest
And enough wood for winter.
"Come on, you ornery beast,"
He muttered.
They plodded on toward home
Pulling the future behind them
Like a plow.

TED THOMPSON

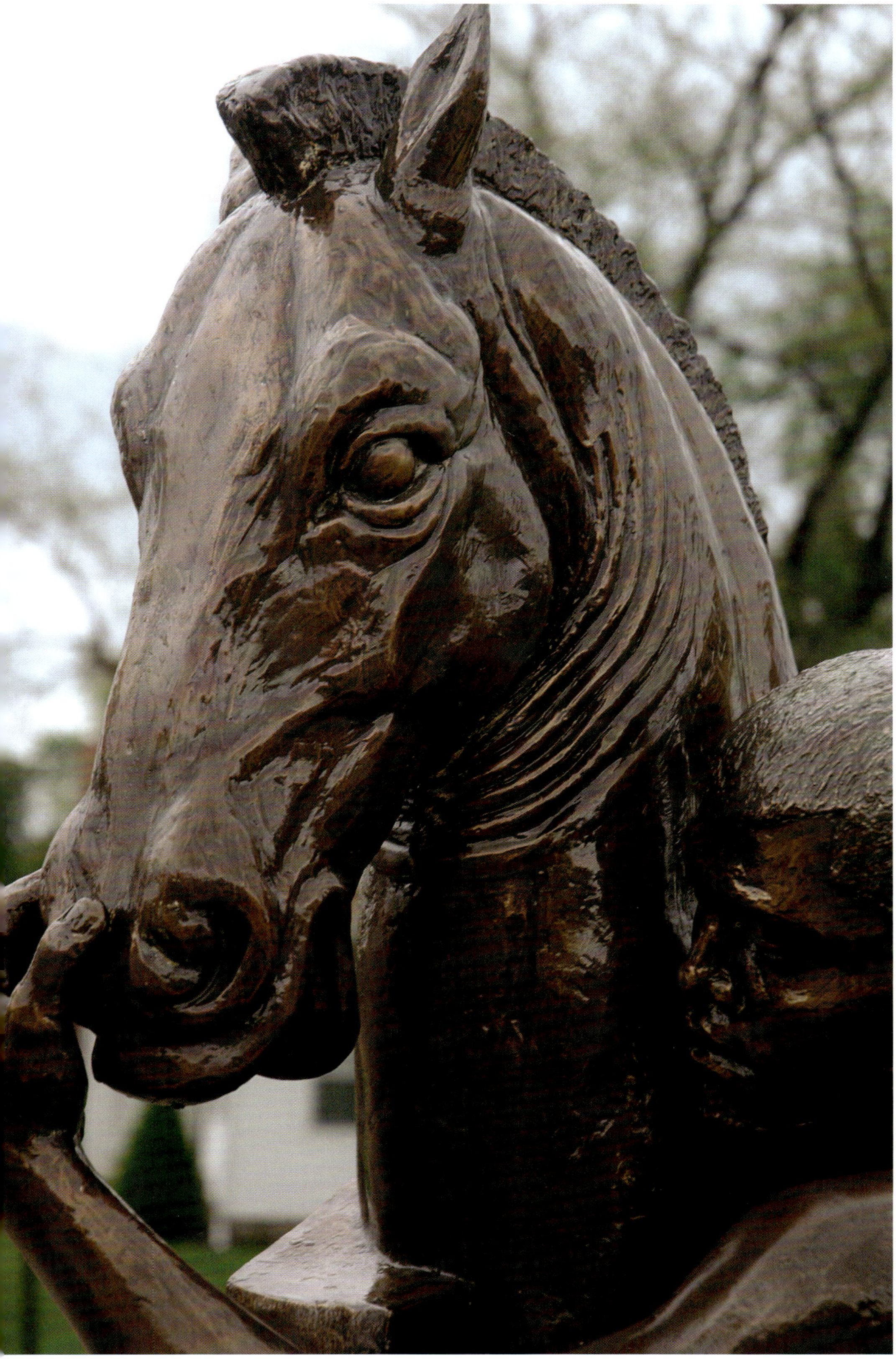

Traveling the Plank Road:
A Working Companionship

SCULPTURE

LEAD ARTIST
Kathleen Scarboro

ASSISTANT ARTISTS
Saul Chavira, Dante DiBartolo

MOSAIC

SIMPLE MOSAIC

15

Cathedral Area

More than any neighborhood I know
Joliet's Cathedral Area attracts walkers
Day and night, in sun and shower.
Maybe it's the busy but basically quiet tree-lined streets
Sometimes crazily criss-crossing in diagonal directions
And curving up and down bluffs and hills.
Perhaps the pedestrians are awed or comforted by
The massive presence of St. Raymond's near Six Corners
Where the Old Plank Road meshes with Ruby and Raynor.
The cathedral's silver pyramidal spire soars upwards
To maybe eight stories and peals at regular intervals
And for weddings, funerals, and holidays.
Also pleasant are the hymns and carols tolled by First Presbyterian
And the campus of St. Francis University
With its five story brick bell towers and four story limestone
Seminary plus the coming and going of students
And the huge gazebo and playground at nearby Preservation Park.
On Halloween or Christmas nights Western Avenue lights up
From Raynor to Center where scores of Victorian houses
Dazzle with decorations but which are equally spectacular
By day with five-color paint, towers, cupolas, stained glass
Windows, beveled glass entryways and wild weather vanes.
But my favorite spot is at Whitney and Buell
A short block from the house here depicted.
Wooded lots sweeping up hills in every direction
Combine with terraced landscaping and an
Assortment of old stately homes, mostly brick
Equally impressive limestone structures, patios, and gazebos.
Vibrations here for me echo from an elegant past
But celebrate a vital present.

JOHN STOBART

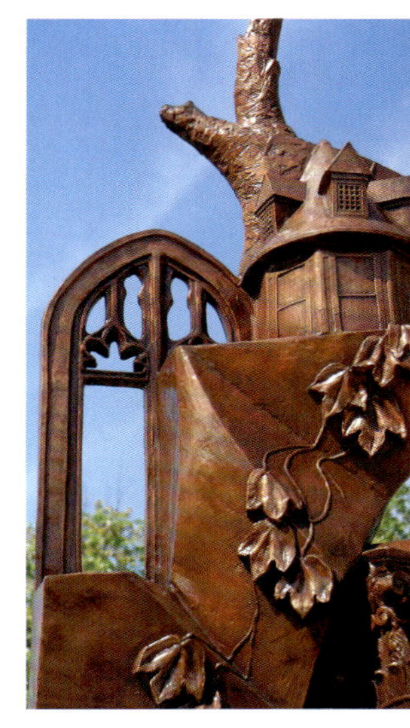

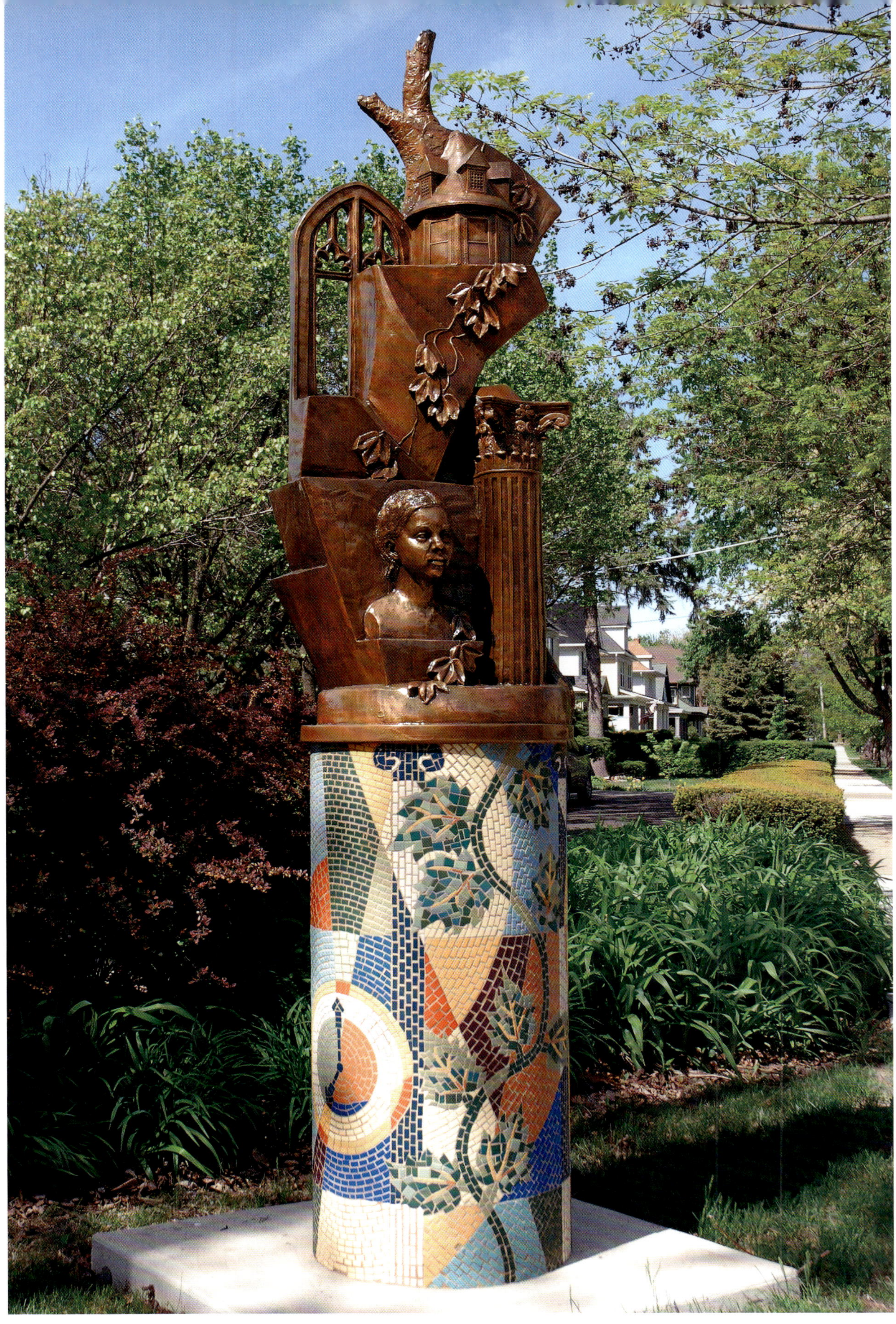

History Clings Like Ivy

SCULPTURE

LEAD ARTIST
Kathleen Scarboro

ASSISTANT ARTIST
Dante DiBartolo, Roger Carlson

MOSAIC

LEAD ARTIST
David Yanchick

Historic Preservation: Our Neighborhood

SCULPTURE

LEAD ARTIST
Kathleen Scarboro

ASSISTANT ARTIST
Dante DiBartolo, Roger Carlson

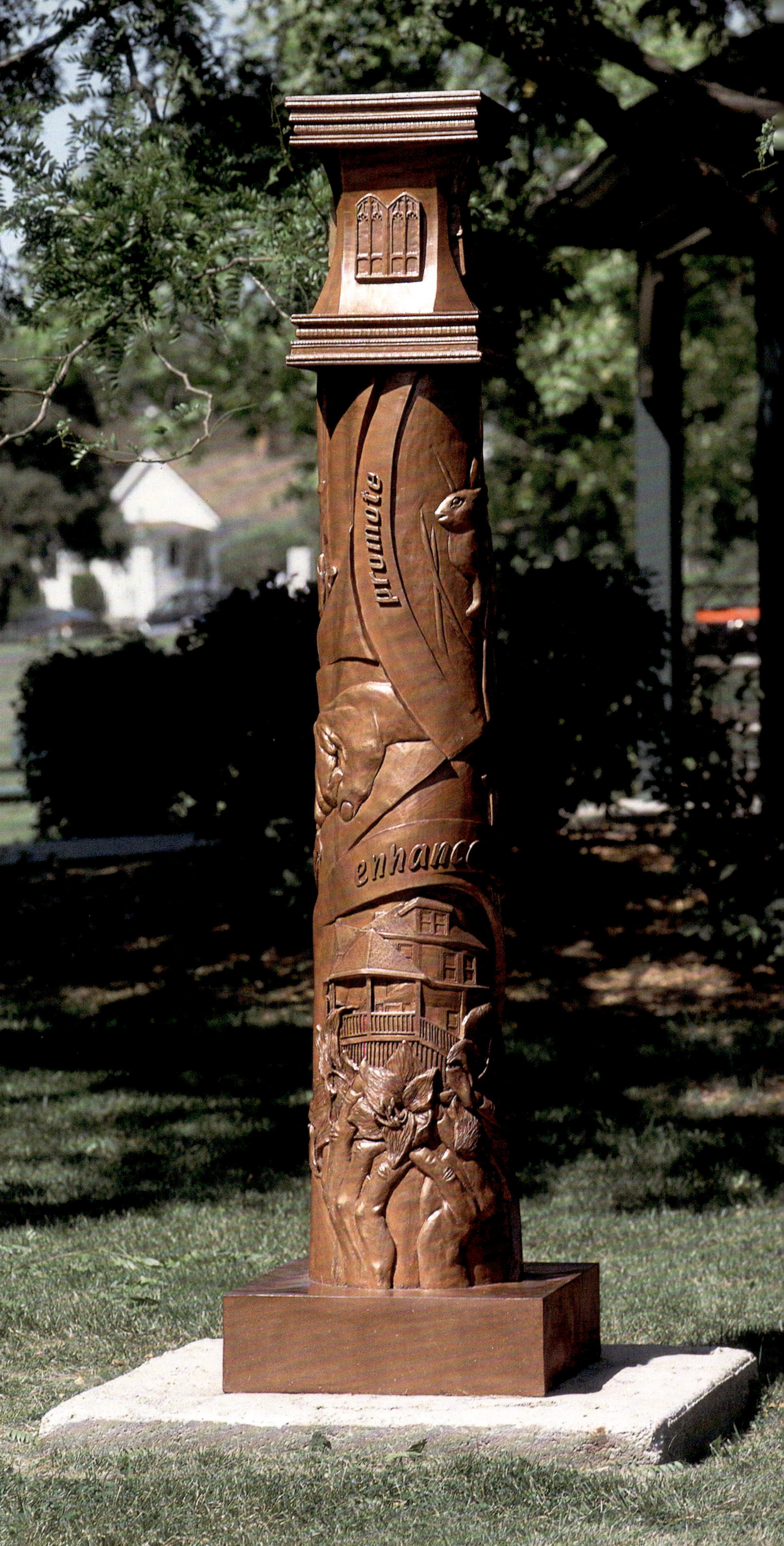

Rejuvenation

What looks like a totem is a beacon.
A head-dress of the four winds beckon,
and so we come. Each epithet a badge
gladly given. We are enchanted, enhanced.
We reach to touch and are taken into held hands, into animal lands.

Each a token.
We kneel, are moved to a promise. As if asked
to promote: to hand-down the holding of hands;
to discover the worth in who we were; to honor
the wonder of who we will become. We breathe in
the lily fingers.

Its scent of cultivation.
And we are filled, fitted for the future.
The emblem of education, the re-leaf, the new
generation, is in a book filled with letters
we wrote to ourselves.

We are refreshed
with texture and substance. Sated by the symbol
that rejoices to shine. A shrine to what was
built and what cannot fall. We are called
to maintain.

A vocation. There is relief
in being remembered. Relief again
in the making, a mold, a map, our every face.
We long to unfold, lay it flat: an atlas
from a map; a blanket from a bedroll. Stretch
to reach each meaning. Read and dream a rest
for its long standing, yet we go round and
round. Dreaming what to cling to, reading how to climb.

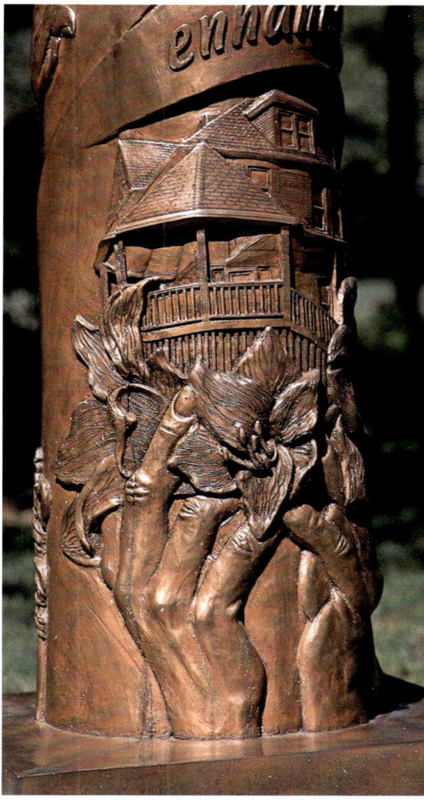

KIM VOLLMER-LAWSON

Dark Good Memories

It's not the shoes. They didn't work
for Mollie, on or off. It was
the running feat that helped her soar
to fame and doom—her running news
of stuff that others wouldn't touch.

Yeah, she was tough, surprising, like
old Abe: Top hat, yet frontier tough
when facing vital tests of will
(way seven score and more years ago)
when a nation fought itself to survive

As One, so homes again would welcome
one and all to sacred space
so long so scarred, where freedom, justice
would live on, inside and out –
Our Mollie Zelco legacy.

EARL VALENTINE FISCHER

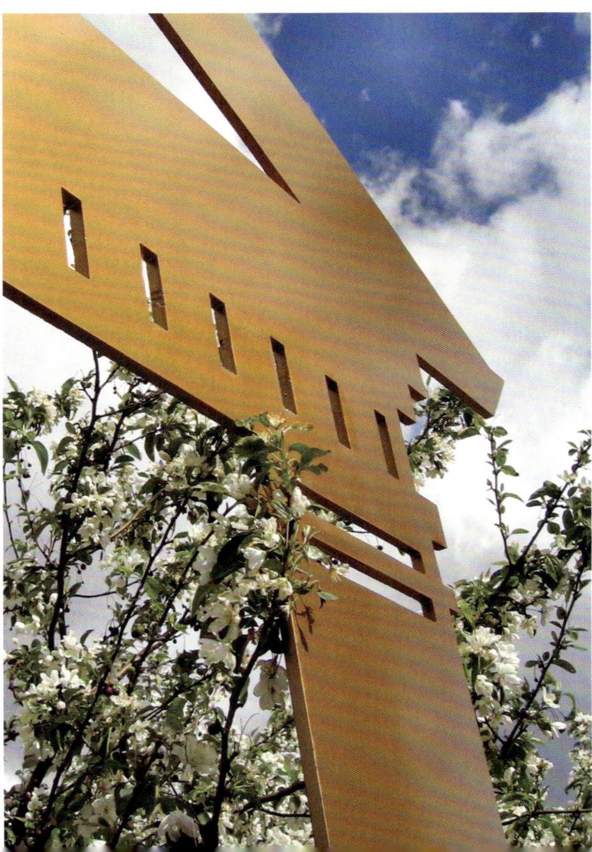

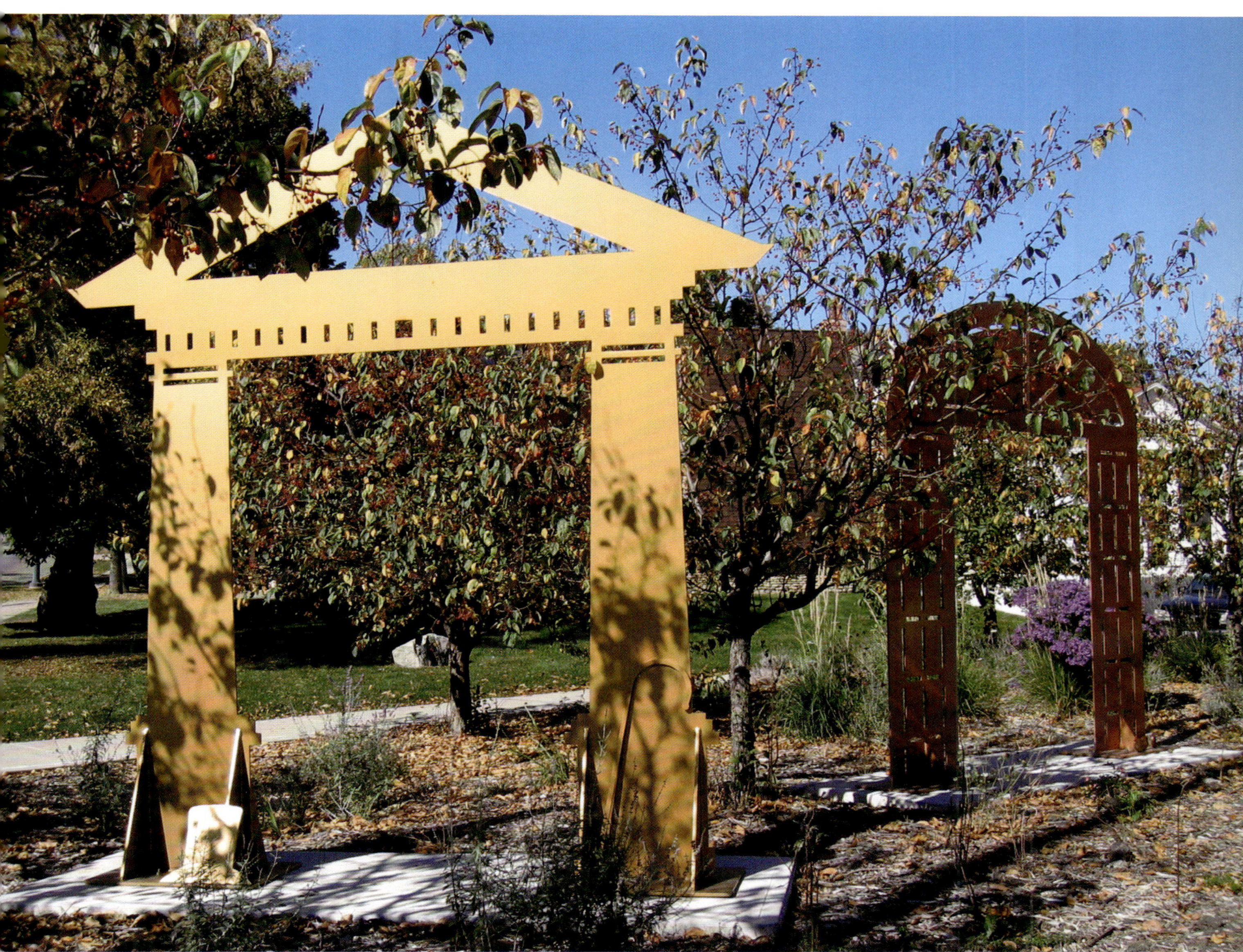

Portals of Buell Avenue

SCULPTURE

LEAD ARTIST
Marsha Lega

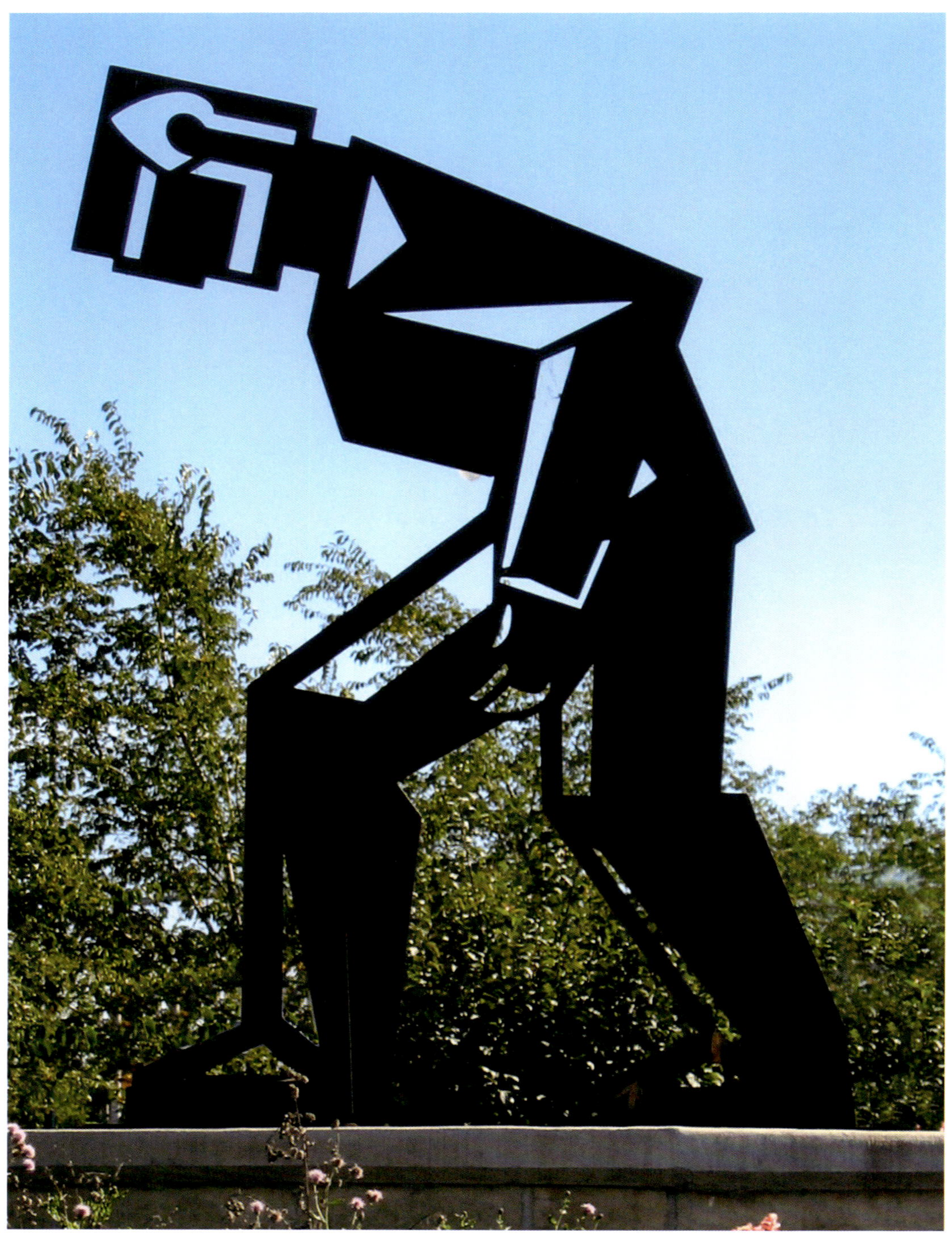

The New Steelman

SCULPTURE

LEAD ARTIST

Marsha Lega

Steelman 2006

Matter is my nemesis
People, places, things are in my way
I am required to move forward
Head down, fists clenched
Slogging long, thrusting hard
I blindly crash obstacles.
No matter what, I overcome!

My ancestors are on display across the street
Creations of Louise Lenz*
As a tribute to science's contributions to civilization
Featured at Chicago's Century of Progress in 1933.
My family is depicted as gentle and gracious.
And evolving from the architecture of Egypt
Including Math and Physics, Agriculture and Engineering

But I have progressed further
I get the job done myself, alone.
I have championed this "City of Steel, City of Stone."
My image is born again age upon age
To appear sometimes Blue, often Gold
Sometimes silver stainless, sometimes rust
To appear on windshield stickers, keychains,
Lunch boxes, on sweatshirts, letter jackets,
Warmups, hoodies, T-shirts, Thank-You notes…
Steelman rules!

JOHN STOBART

*A JTHS alum. Her tableau and another steelman, "The Puddler," are on view on the first floor, across from the principal's office.

Egret

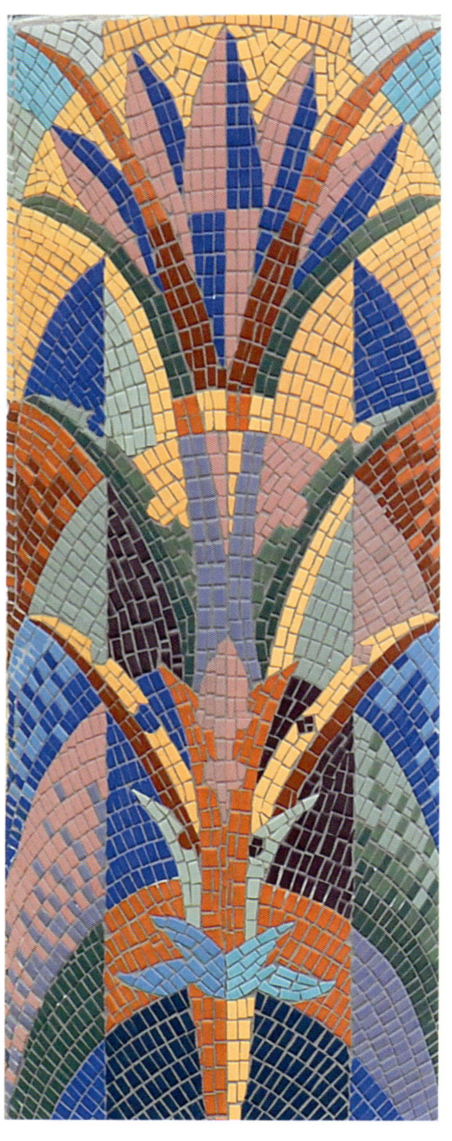

Lank wader
Solitary hunter,
Quietly eyeing the water
Beneath your arrow beak,
A white tallness among the reeds.

Noisy socialite,
Exchanging gossip in
The gathering evening shadows,
Necking your nest-mate,
Happy in your hundreds,
A feathered frenzy of flocking.

My little schizoid,
Have you sought an analyst
About your dual nature,
Or do you merely accept it
Like the sunrise
That beckons you rise once more
For your morning commute.

TED THOMPSON

nature

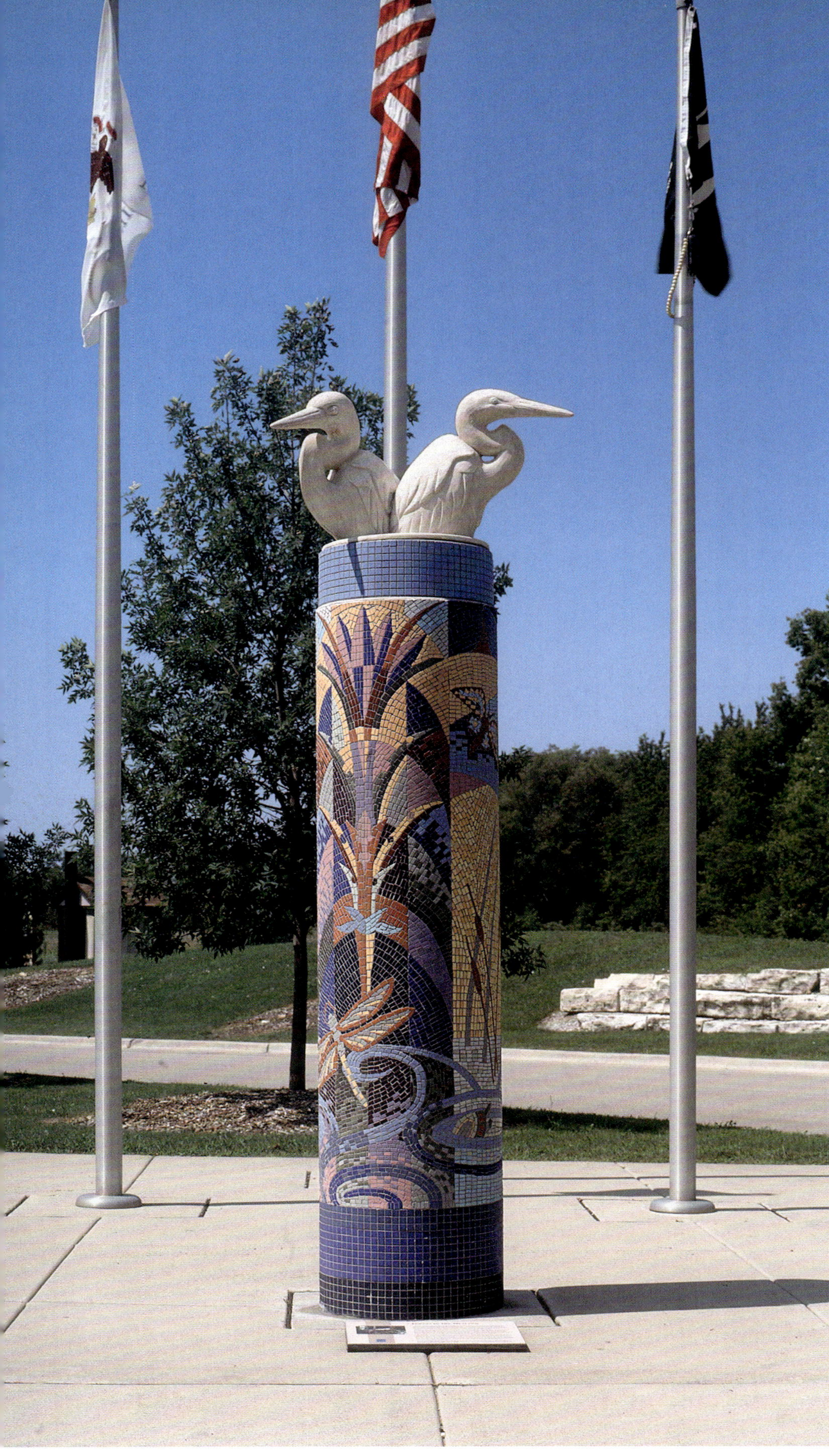

Egrets in the Wetland

SCULPTURE

LEAD ARTIST
Kathleen Farrell

ASSISTANT ARTIST
Dante DiBartolo

MOSAIC

LEAD ARTIST
Kathleen Scarboro

The Barn Owl and the Moon

At night we tumble to sleep under rafters,
beneath the moon. Bats' breath against our lips.
The barn owl and the moon.
A scream, a snore, a hiss, a click, a scratch.
Duets of eyes, aglow, on fire at night.
Roost in silos or steeples through daylight.
Come dark, then pounce: voles, bats, mice, crickets, shrews.
Your heart-shaped face, talons, and tawny skin.
My crescent arc—waxing—all marrow, pearl.
The barn owl and the moon.
Fixed in the sky. A scythe. Afraid to cut.
We hide. This flash might blind and talons strip.

It's dark. A drumbeat of feathers scales up
my spine. Rapt, out-of-breath, we tilt, take wing.
You clasp a shell of skin. I shed more light
tucked between claw and claw. Rise above earth:
    the barn owl and the moon.

ELISE PASCHEN

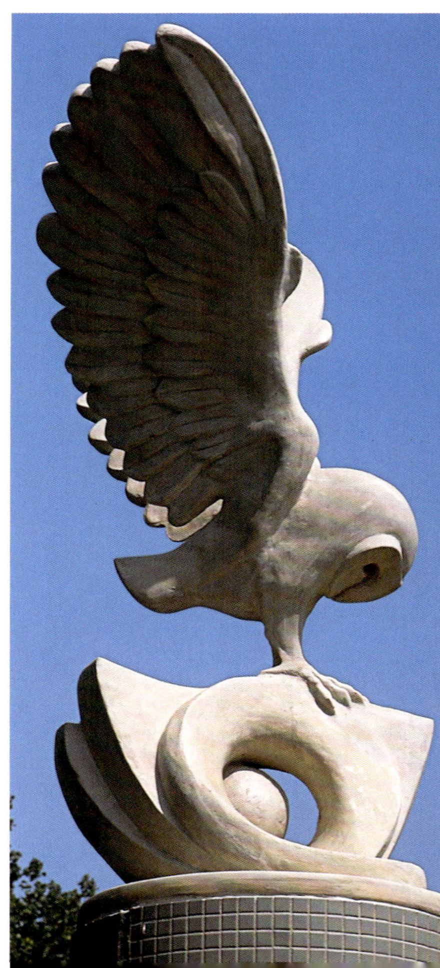

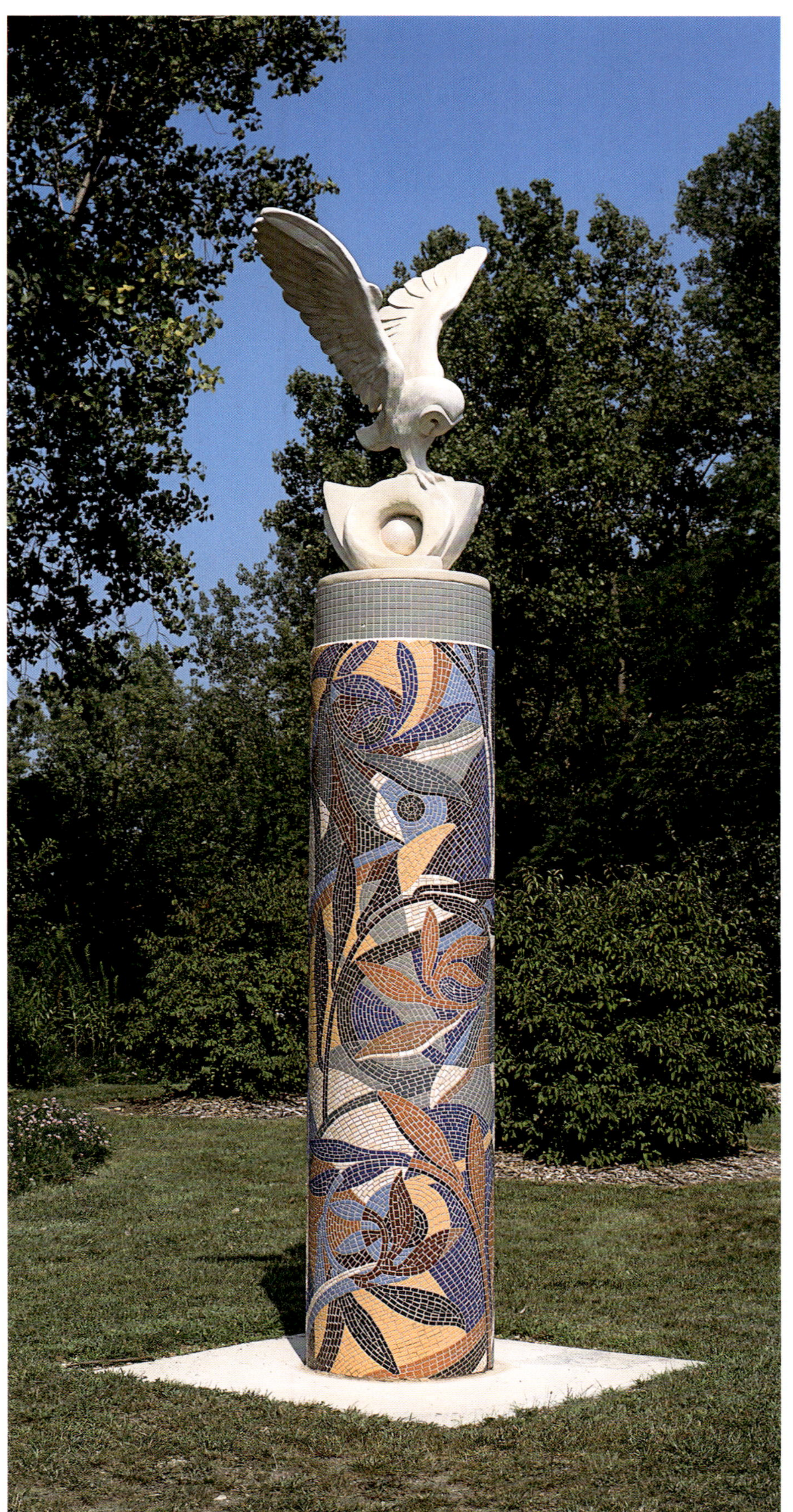

The Barn Owl and the Moon

SCULPTURE

LEAD ARTIST
Kathleen Scarboro

ASSISTANT ARTIST
Sarah Furst, Dante DiBartolo

MOSAIC

LEAD ARTIST
Kathleen Scarboro

Red Tail Hawk: The Nature of Our Neighborhood

SCULPTURE

LEAD ARTIST
Sarah Furst

ASSISTANT ARTIST
Dante DiBartolo

MOSAIC

LEAD ARTIST
Sarah Furst

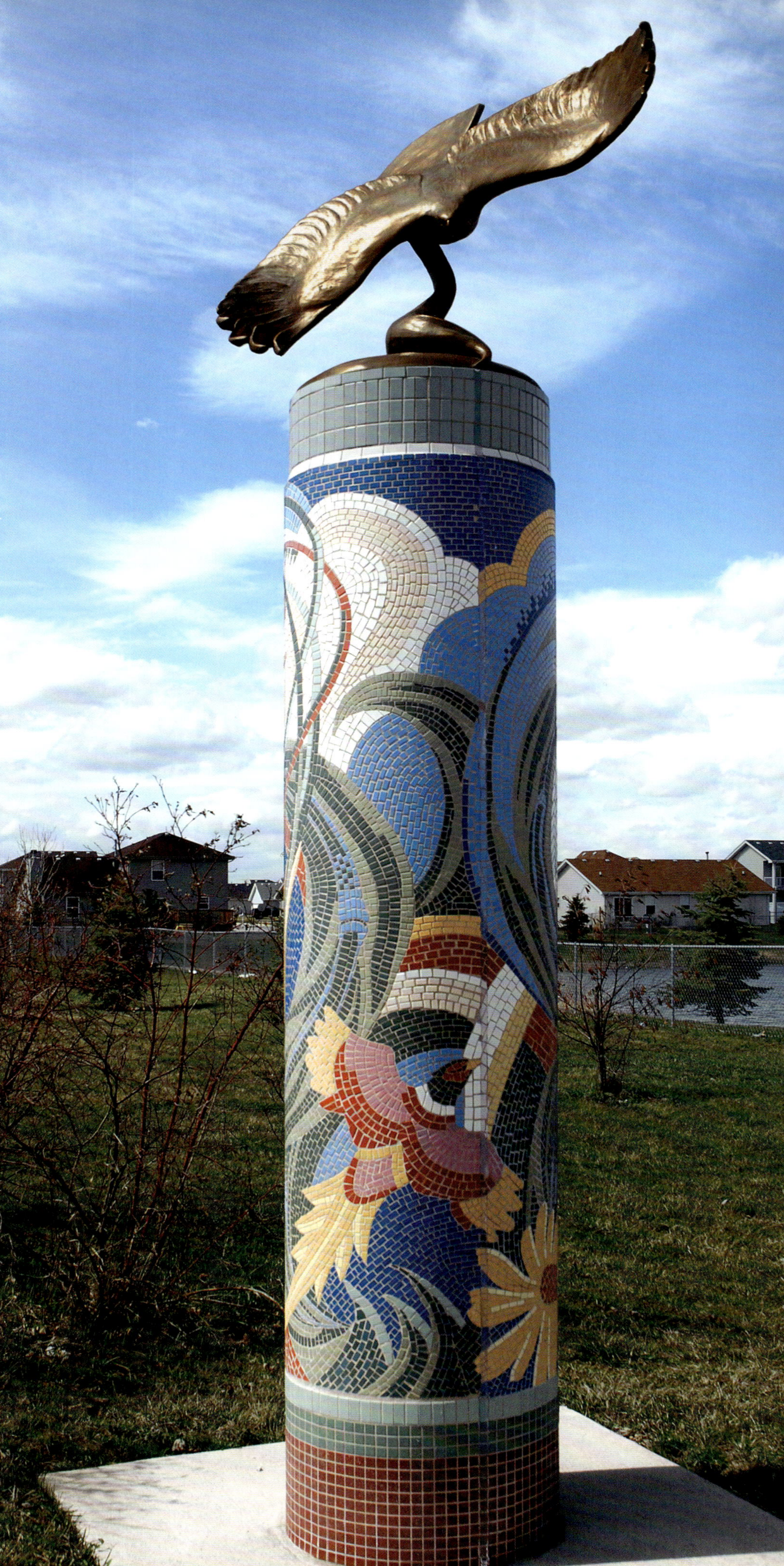

The Hawk

Wings blessed with poise and grace,
The hawk soars in cerulean space.

Oblivious to human lives,
The hawk survives.

By night nested on a limb
Gorgeous feathers no longer ruffled by the wind.

Talons pointed like a blade,
The call of the hawk does fade,

Drowned by traffic and passers-by,
The hawk has evolved to float on high,

Wings blessed with poise and grace
The hawk lives above the human race,

Oblivious, it seems to human lives,
The hawk survives and thrives.

AMY OUTLAND

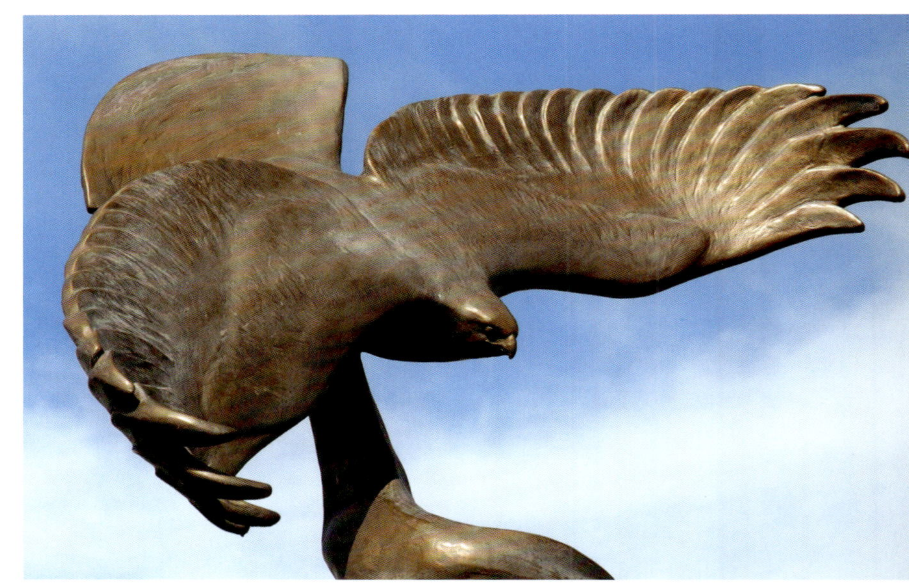

Hail, Splendidissima!

Imported for the fun of it—the chase,
old times—the Vulpes vulpes whirls, enjoys
a quick look back. Of fourteen fox types, "ace"
here has the most close cousins. Now the boys
in the old guys' network number forty-six
sly clans all joined as gentlemen of the red coat.
Viz., Vulpes Vulpes Vulpes (what a fix:
all three in one). Plus, sculpted here, please note
the Vulpes Vulpes Splendidissima.
Oh, may that scientific name be praised
(poetic plunder pick)—fortissima.
Correct term for this fox or not, it's aptly phrased.
The hunted, now the hunter, has a tale
to flash: he's ready, waiting for "all hail."

EARL VALENTINE FISCHER

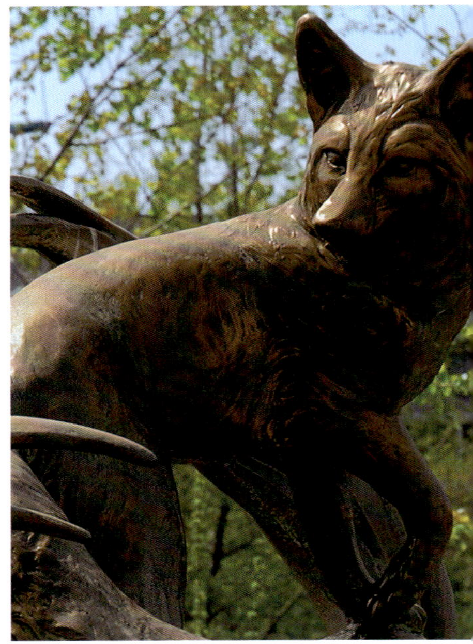

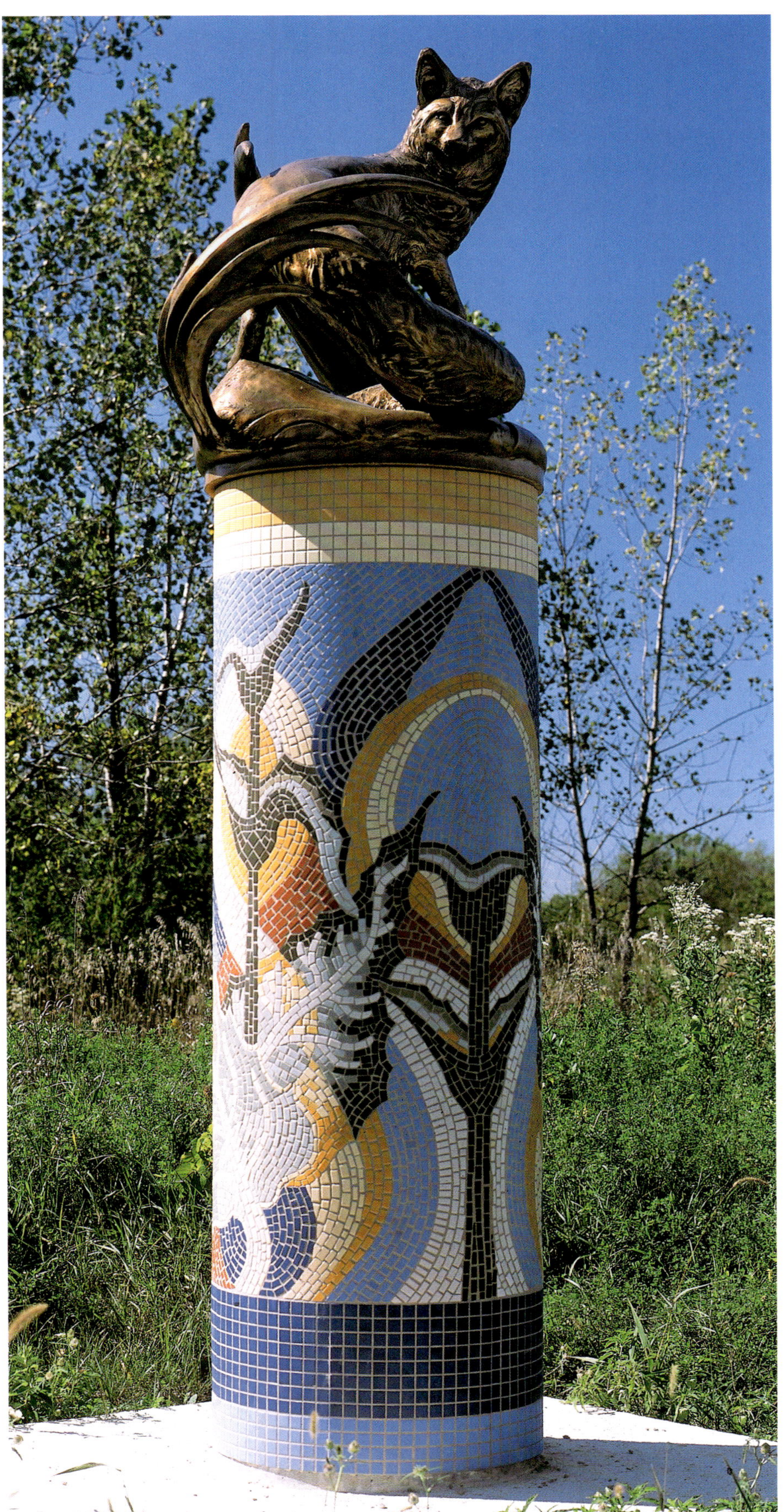

Fox in Cattails

SCULPTURE

LEAD ARTIST
Sarah Furst

MOSAIC

LEAD ARTIST
Sarah Furst

Nature: The Flow of Life

SCULPTURE

LEAD ARTIST
Sarah Furst

MOSAIC

LEAD ARTIST
Sarah Furst

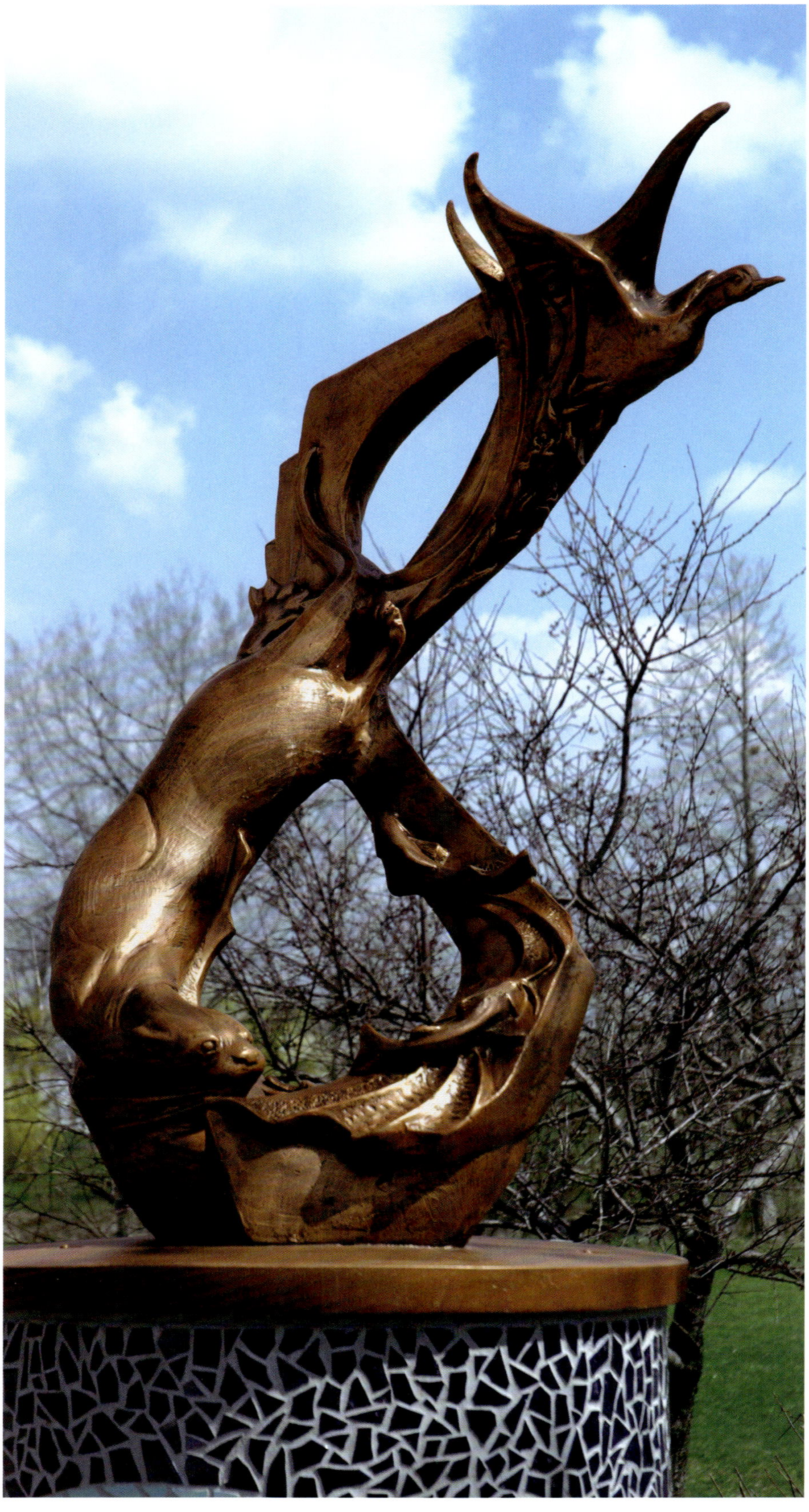

The Flow

Gentle little river
    DuPage
lapping lush wetlands
'neath a canopy of trees.

Otters cavort
    fearless
        frolicksome
            friendly
while the wood duck
shyly shows reserve.
The red-eared slider
scrapes the strand
with speed impressive
for a turtle.
A kingfisher dives
while fish flash
beneath the surface.
Catfish troll for
submerged treasures.

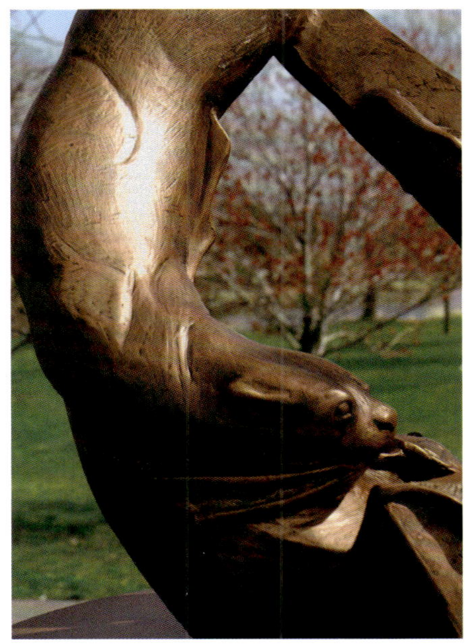

Flowers
    of the yellow flag
        flutter
while the flow of life
moves with the current.

NANCY FISCHER

Touching

With a small smile
And firm embrace
This gentle grandma, grannie, or nana
Epitomizes the blend of grace and power
Desirable to nurture humanity.
She provides clues to universal mysteries
Or real and ideal problems
By reading stories and singing songs,
Posing riddles, exploring myths.
Her audience is a young boy
Who knows that she knows
What he wants and needs
To get along for a while
Through laughing and loving talks and play
Sprinkled with scares and tears and happiness
Experienced and remembered
Imperfectly unto eternity

JOHN STOBART

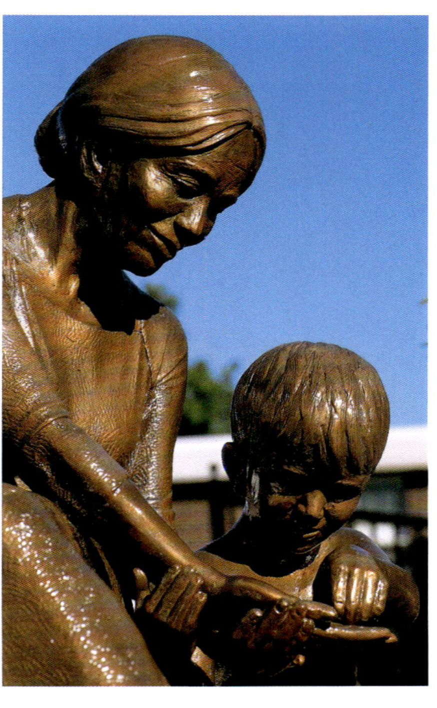

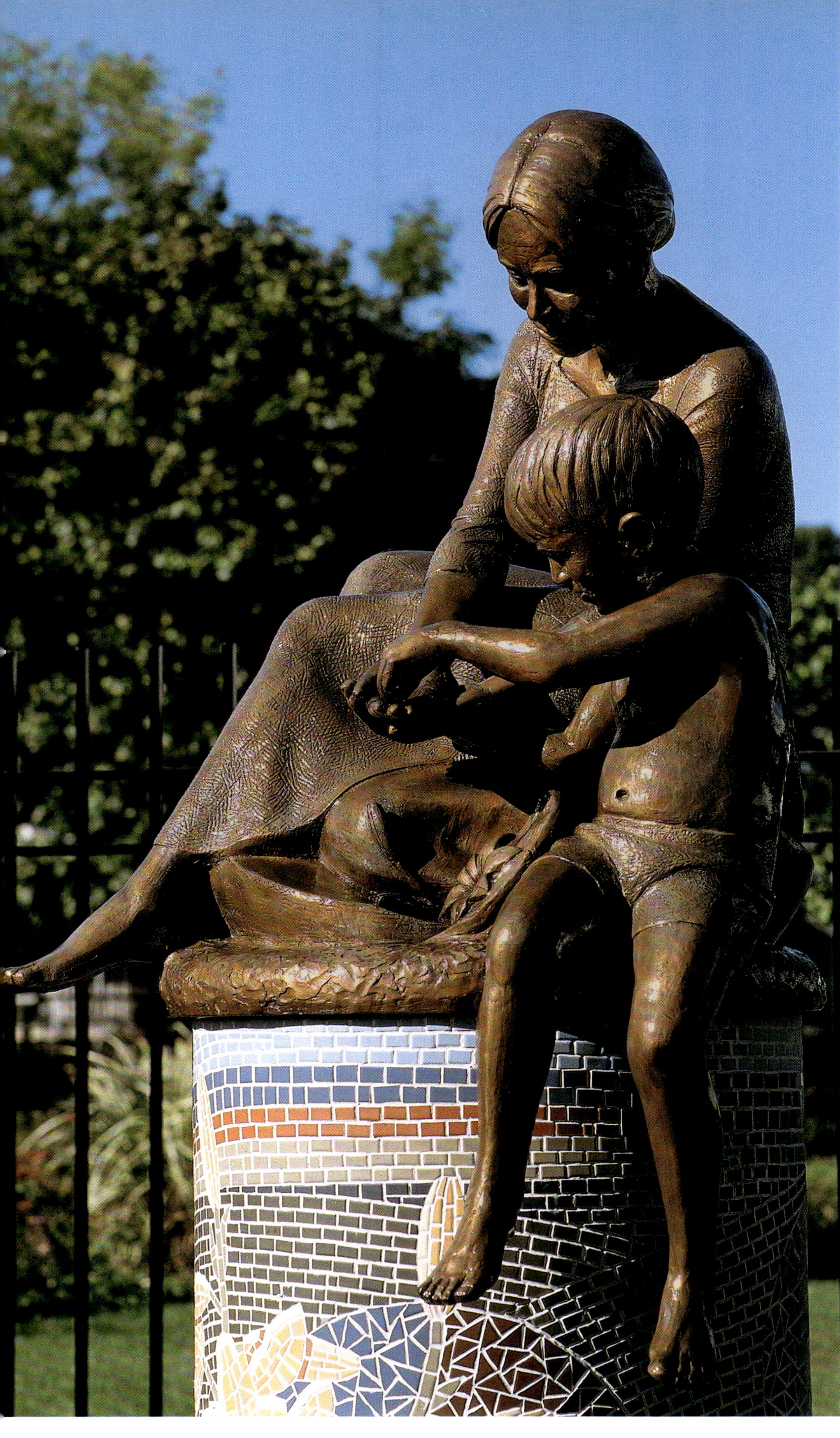

allegory

Wisdom: A Grandmother and Grandchild

SCULPTURE

LEAD ARTIST
Sarah Furst

ASSISTANT ARTIST
Saul Chavira

MOSAIC

LEAD ARTIST
Saul Chavira

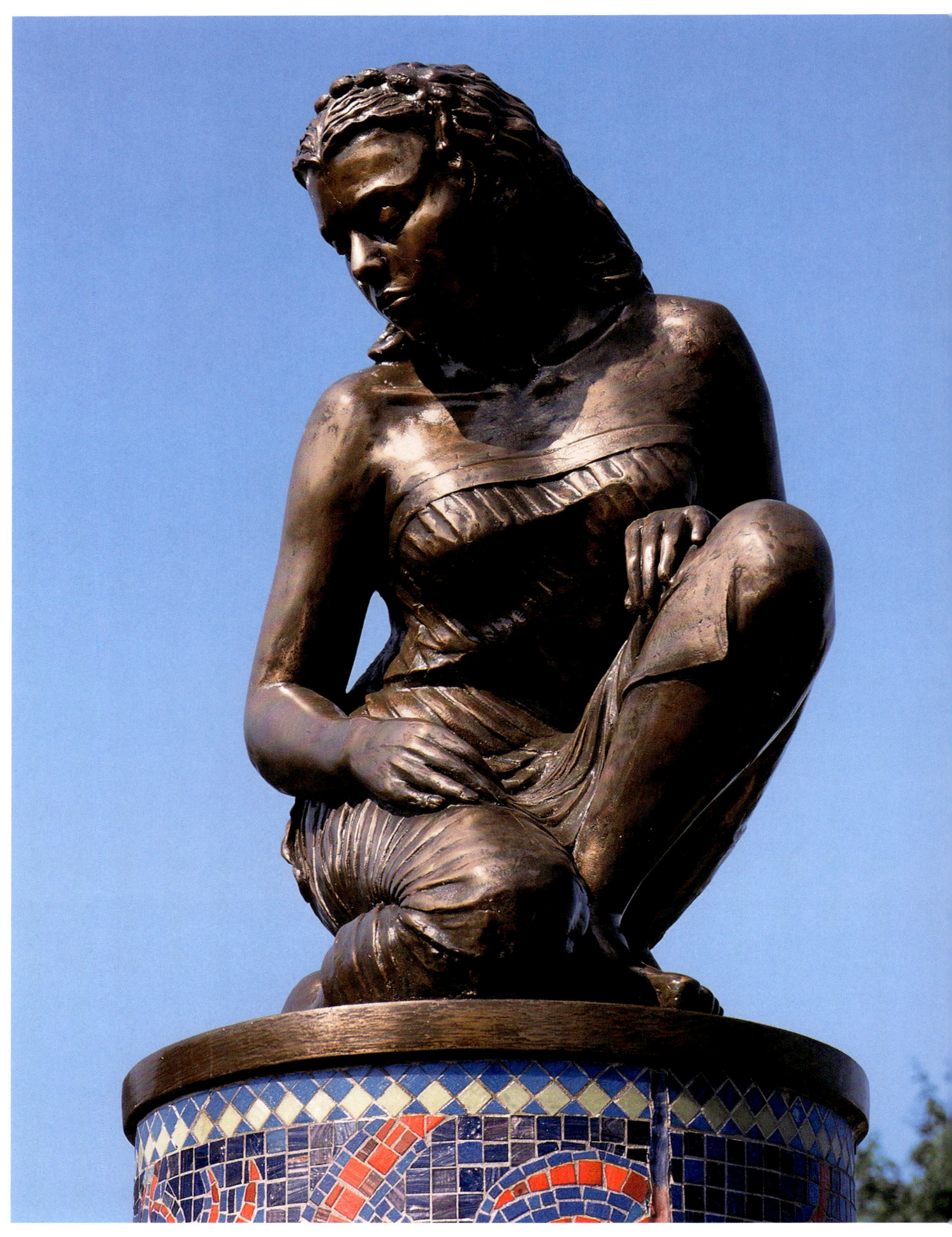

Mother Nature

SCULPTURE

LEAD ARTIST
Kathleen Farrell

ASSISTANT ARTISTS
Dante DiBartolo, Sarah Furst

MOSAIC

LEAD ARTIST
Andrea Rountree

Cold Spring

Mornings now, I watch
the huge old black-armed trees
and wait for them to pull new handkerchief-
like leaves from their top branches
to wave above the shingled houses
into the sky

in this early cold spring
their limbs all crack and creak.

Beneath oak shadows
crocus bulbs crack peels of skin
stretching from the black earth sleep
toward a wild snap of light
to crown themselves
purple, yellow, orange, and red
in this coronation spring

it's been a long winter.
Mornings now, the stairs still cold
beneath my feet
I feel a new flowering
of pain tug in my hip
and twine dark leaves along my spine.
When I stretch in the morning sun
I hear joints crack and creak.
Have I aged in the night?
or grown new again
like the pulled half of a wishbone moon
fleshing round in the bare sky, a growing thing
Mornings now
my bones all ache and sing.

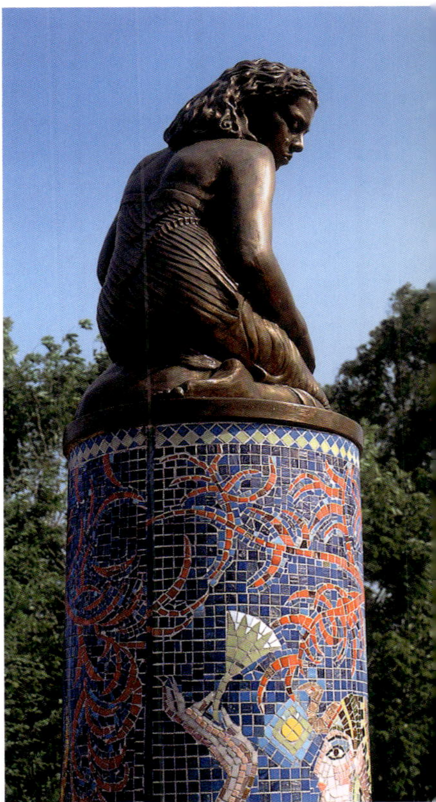

JULIE PARSON-NESBITT

The Tiller of the Earth

My grandfather's face is Mississippi Delta
he tills. His variegated wrinkles
irrigate trenches for bumper yields, I once
asked what he tilled : « Hard land, boy, hard land. »
Truth is his tears were dry and prayer,
in fact, waters roots of hope. Now at 63,
I see my image in tilled mirrors of grandfather's
furrowed identity. Like him, I have no tears and
poems wash down canals meandering
my countenance. I live for this cartographed
geography of skin that offers myth as harvest.
I am born and will surely die as a farmer.
My body is the only acreage I lease;
till for architecture of crops I dream.

STERLING D. PLUMPP

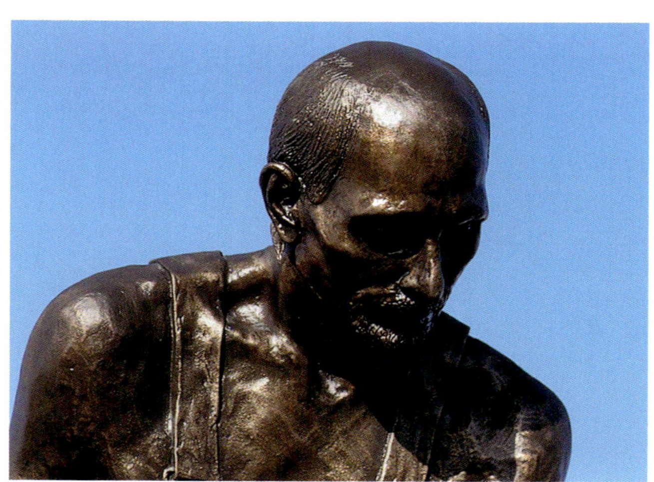

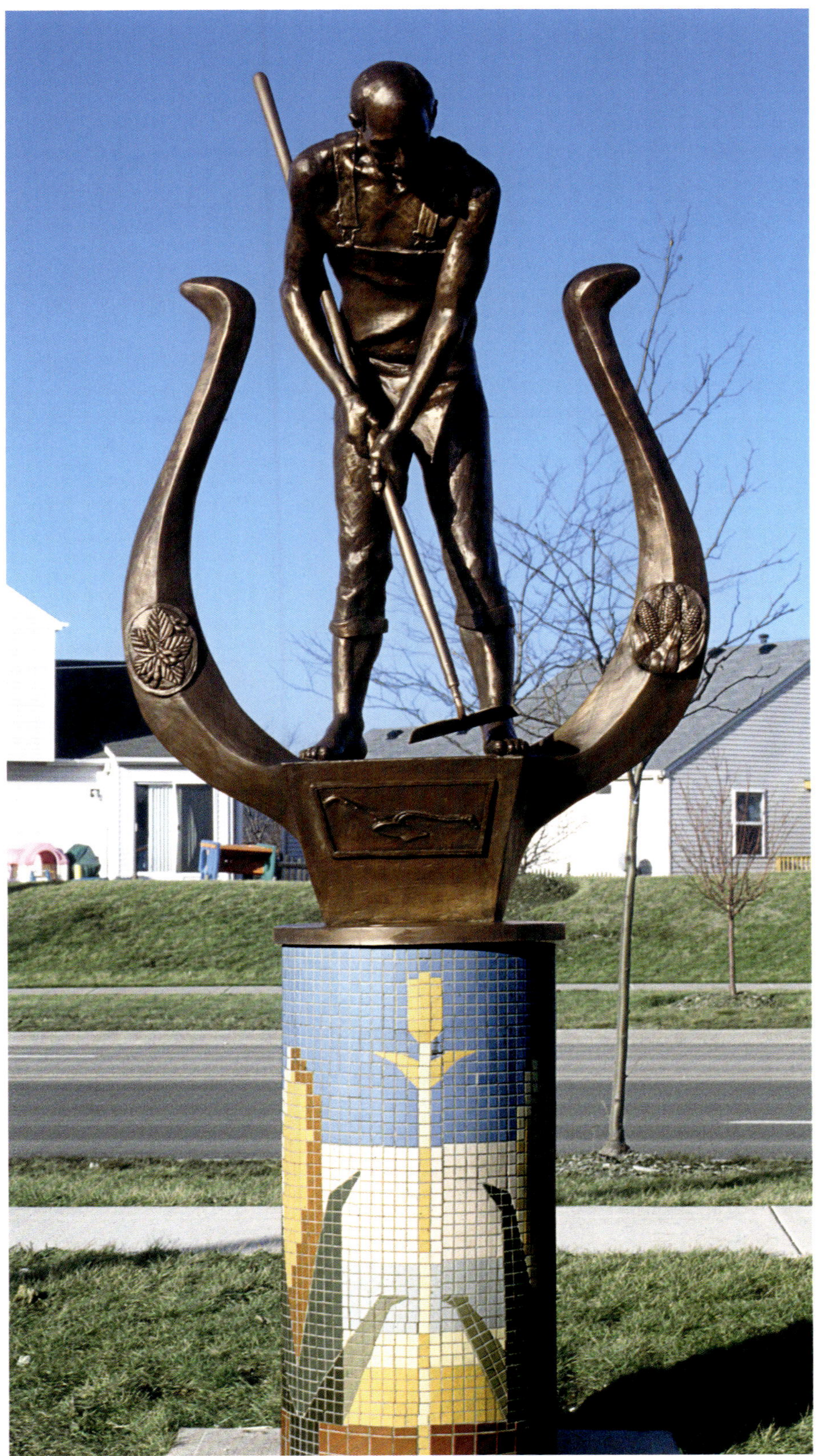

The Tiller of the Earth

SCULPTURE

LEAD ARTIST
Kathleen Scarboro

ASSISTANT ARTISTS
Dante DiBartolo,
Kelly Yadura-Gallaher

MOSAIC

LEAD ARTIST
David Yanchick

Spirit of the River

SCULPTURE

LEAD ARTIST
Kathleen Farrell

ASSISTANT ARTISTS
Dante DiBartolo,
Annick Bailly,
Saul Chavira

MOSAIC

LEAD ARTIST
Saul Chavira

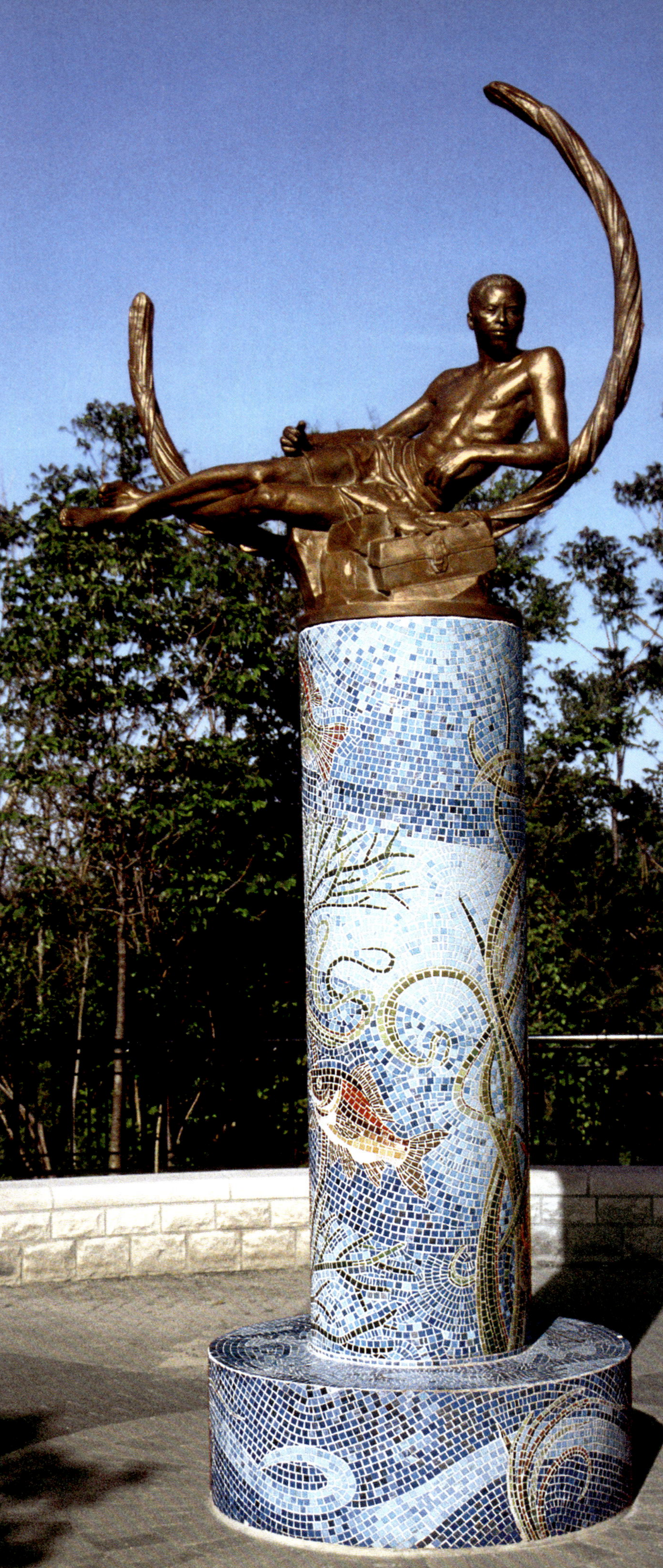

Spirit Sonnet

On a quilt of sea stones, our hero is afloat.
An arc of wands, a twist of river
Reeds, whether wood or weed,
His nest a vessel, this wreath a boat.

He is raised, ablaze, a silent sage
His sun-soaked skin, age will not graze.

A dangle of dinner, petals
Of feathered fins, are on his lap.
Even nature's tangle is regal,
A grand stance, relaxed.

Our eyes dine on this glowing soul.
Lord and guard of his river below.

He is king in a kerchief, spirit guide,
His lashes lace this country-side.
A solitary sojourn is caught, gilded still;
Yet, his eyes swim like stones on a live sea quilt.

KIM VOLLMER-LAWSON

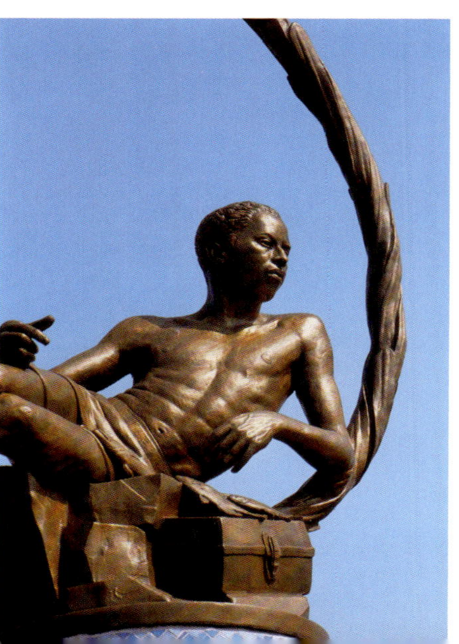

By Any Other Name

Blake's rose was symbolic without a doubt
Sublimating some odd sexual thorn;
And gathering rosebuds while they're still about
Keeps Herrick's virgins from being forlorn.
The rose is a poetic tradition
When sweet love, youth, and beauty they tout,
But it's not quite supporting sedition
If I contrarily want to point out

That this waif, who is reaching in wonder
His immediate desire to possess,
May find when it's full in his grasp
That he's made an indelible blunder.
Once in hand, it's loved so much the less.
His quickly plucked pleasure poisons like an asp.

TED THOMPSON

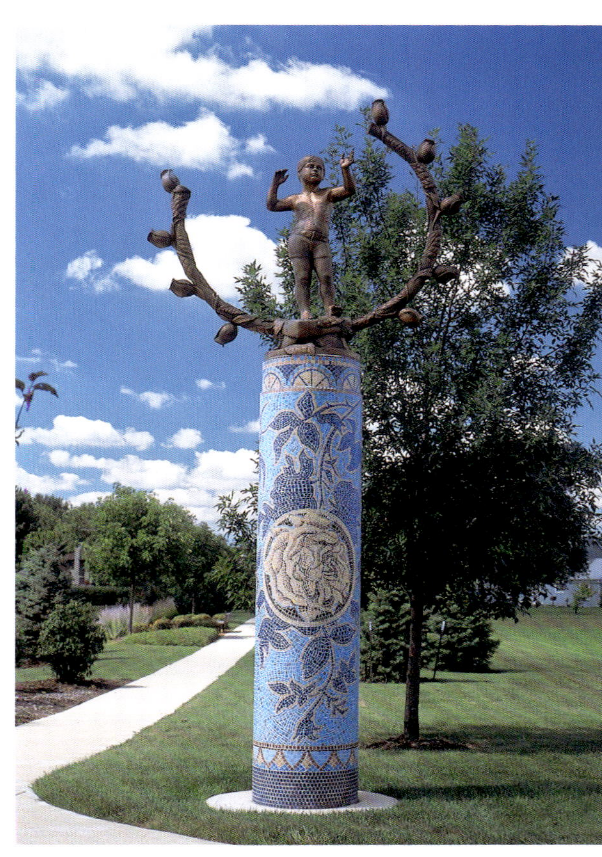

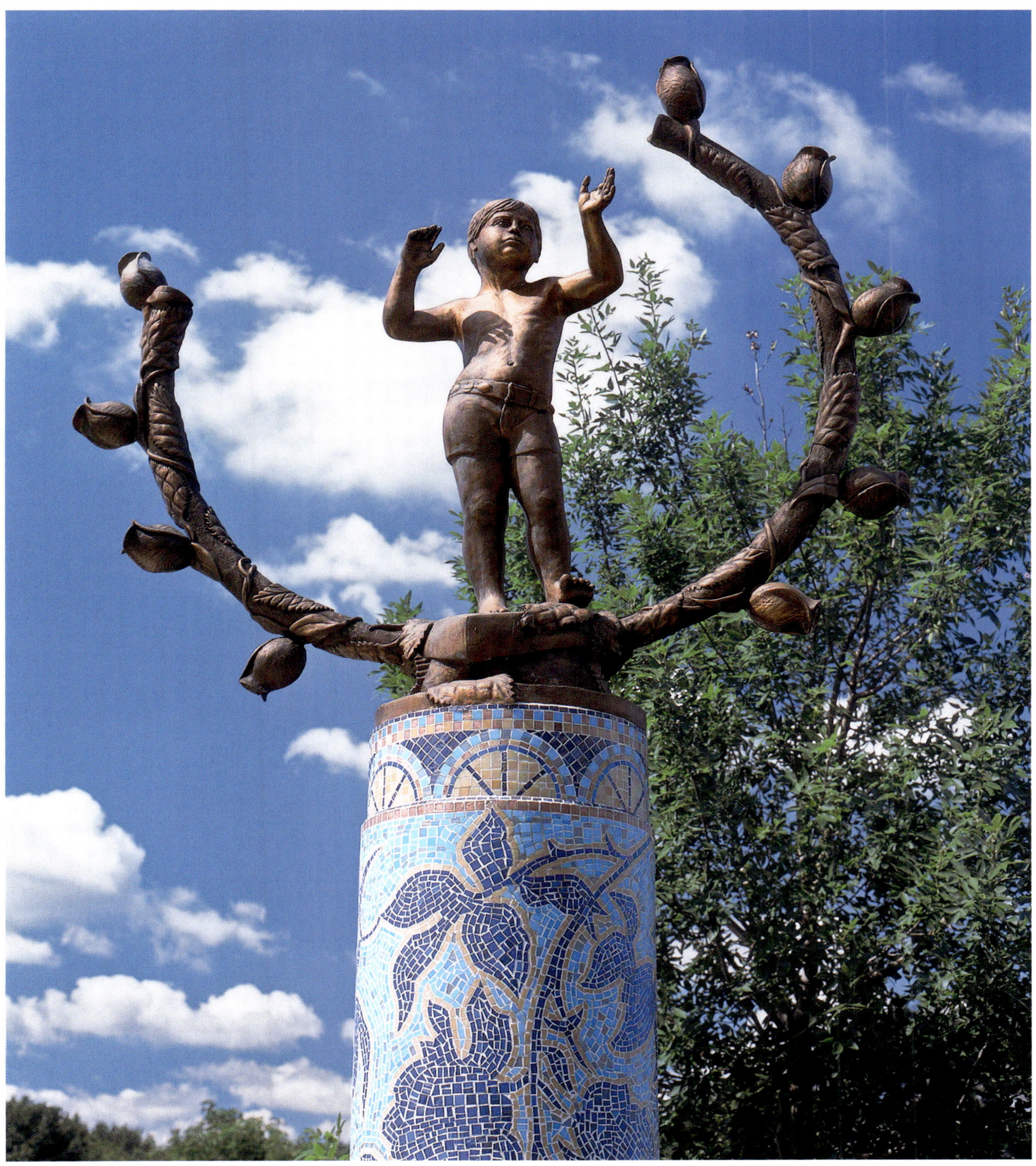

The Boy and the Rose

SCULPTURE

LEAD ARTIST
Kathleen Farrell

ASSISTANT ARTISTS
Dante DiBartolo, Sarah Furst

MOSAIC

LEAD ARTIST
Andrea Rountree

An Informed Mind Can Make Better Choices

SCULPTURE

LEAD ARTIST
Kathleen Farrell

ASSISTANT ARTISTS
Dante DiBartolo, Annick Bailly, Roger Carlson

MOSAIC

SIMPLE MOSAIC

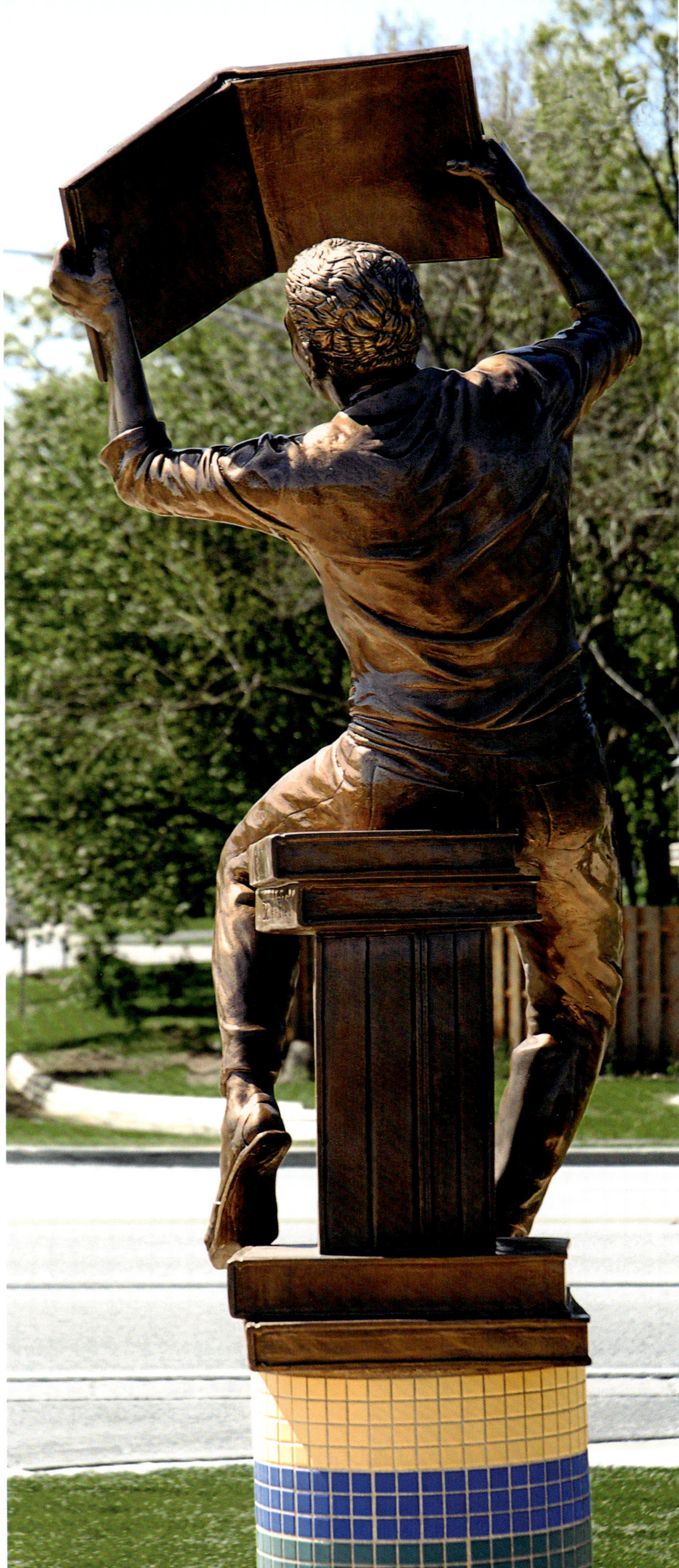

29

An Informed Mind

shoulders strain to hoist ten thousand words
above the head in military press
reading one leaden page
one cavernous sentence
one vaporous word at a time
demands sinewy intellect
without hands to pry page from page
words wiggle into spiritually coarse space
neck craned angular eyes brusquely intent
warrant terse respect
inspect
like passengers through airport security
the galvanization
of mercurial meaning

GEORGE DAVID MILLER

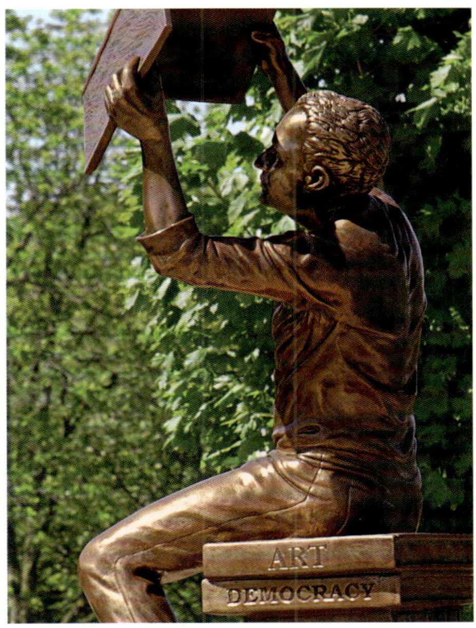

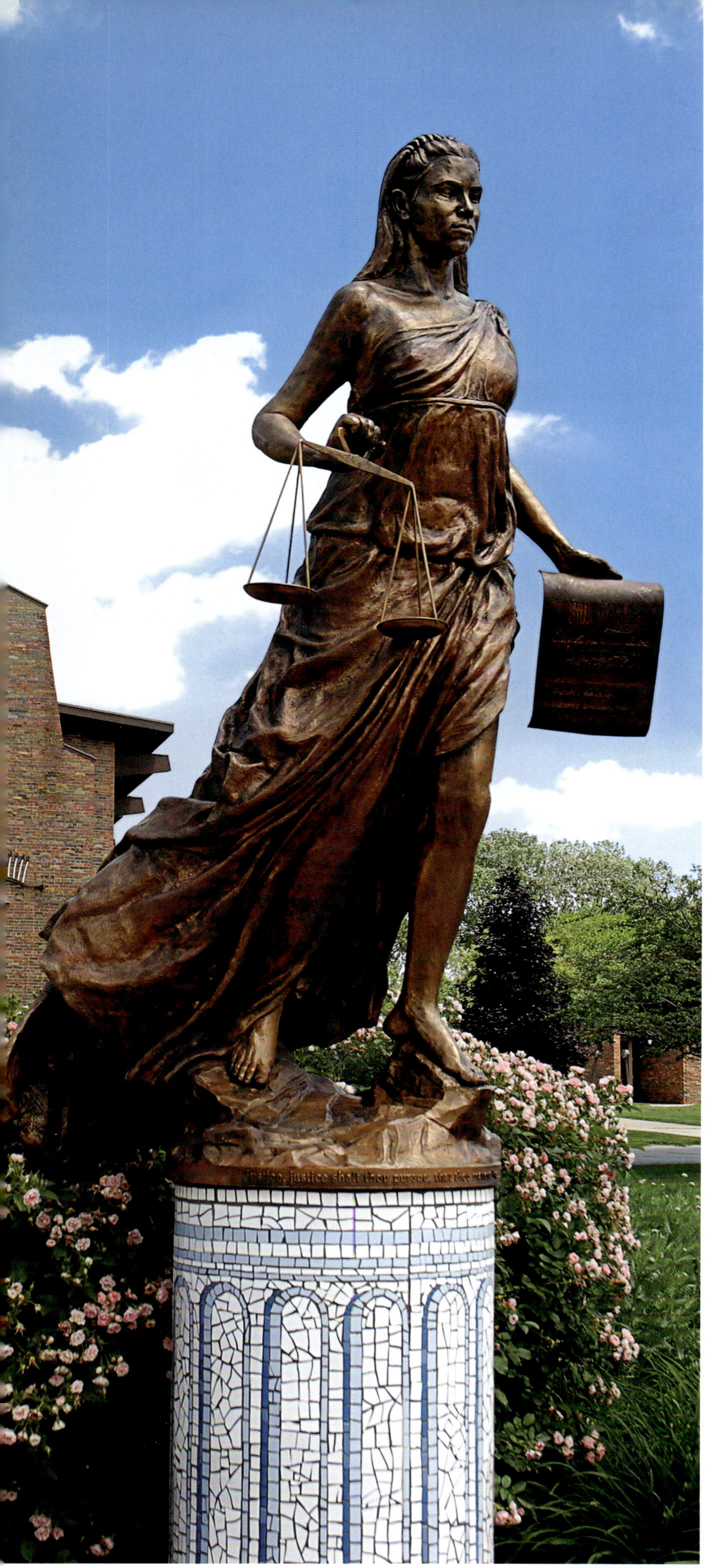

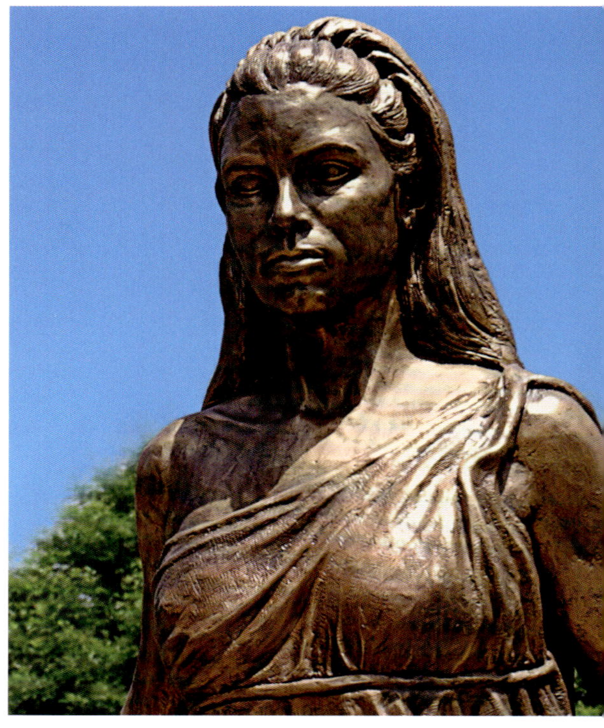

Justice

SCULPTURE

LEAD ARTIST
Kathleen Farrell

ASSISTANT LEAD ARTIST
Dante DiBartolo, David Standifer, Annick Bailly

MOSAIC

LEAD ARTIST
Ilario Silva

Conviction

A year after the trial,
Midnight,
And we lunged over the wire,
Defying the posted rule or law,
POOL CLOSES AT TEN
She yanked off her skirt
revealing the bright mouth of the wound.

She had always reminded me of Athena, long legs and arms muscled
from banging chisels into granite
or wrestling clay into Art.
Could such strength and grace be killed?
I couldn't imagine, but I saw her body,
Draped in white and still, her eyes opened
but glazed blank by morphine,
and I heard the doctor tell that death was expected shortly.

But, at trial, I gloried at the survival of Justice.
I saw her eyes lock on his
As she pointed her arm, her dagger,
At his chest and intoned, "Him…!"

Though he is caged now, far away,
I know his wolf eyes haunt her,
But, for now, I watch her swim
up and down the pool,
her torso slicing through,
Turning back flips, kicking off,
And meeting the water head on
with conviction.

WHITNEY KURTZ-OGILVIE

Think Even This

To think even this will end
the rhythm of exchange, the roaring.
We are deaf forever, living as we do
at its heart. It is all-
we are all-vulnerable
plucked and singular
incapable of even the silent hum,

if it was only as simple as carbon,
as a lifetime, as what runs
through this constant
evaporation,

this slow trickle to extinction

and then this miracle
the tree, the man,
the hot shower.

M. AUFOCHS GILLESPIE

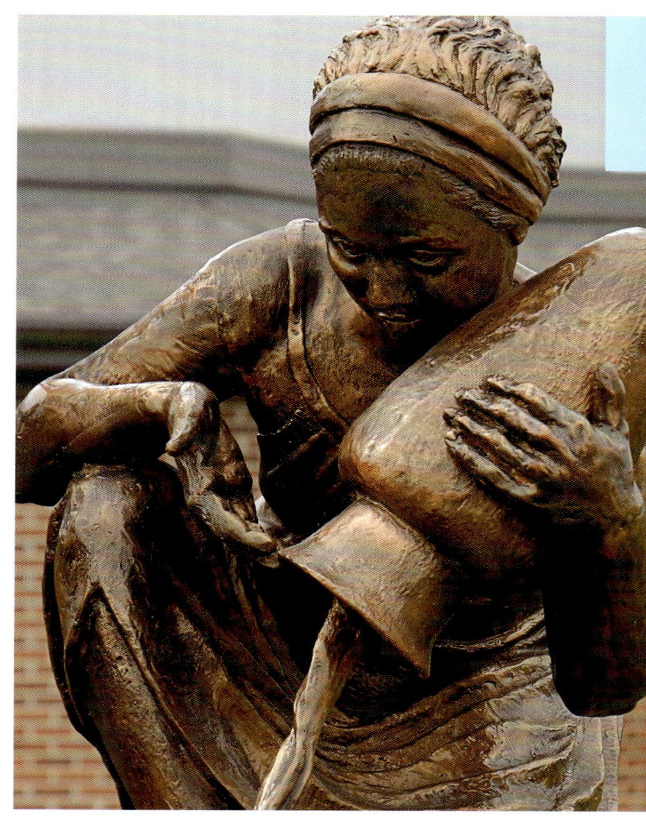

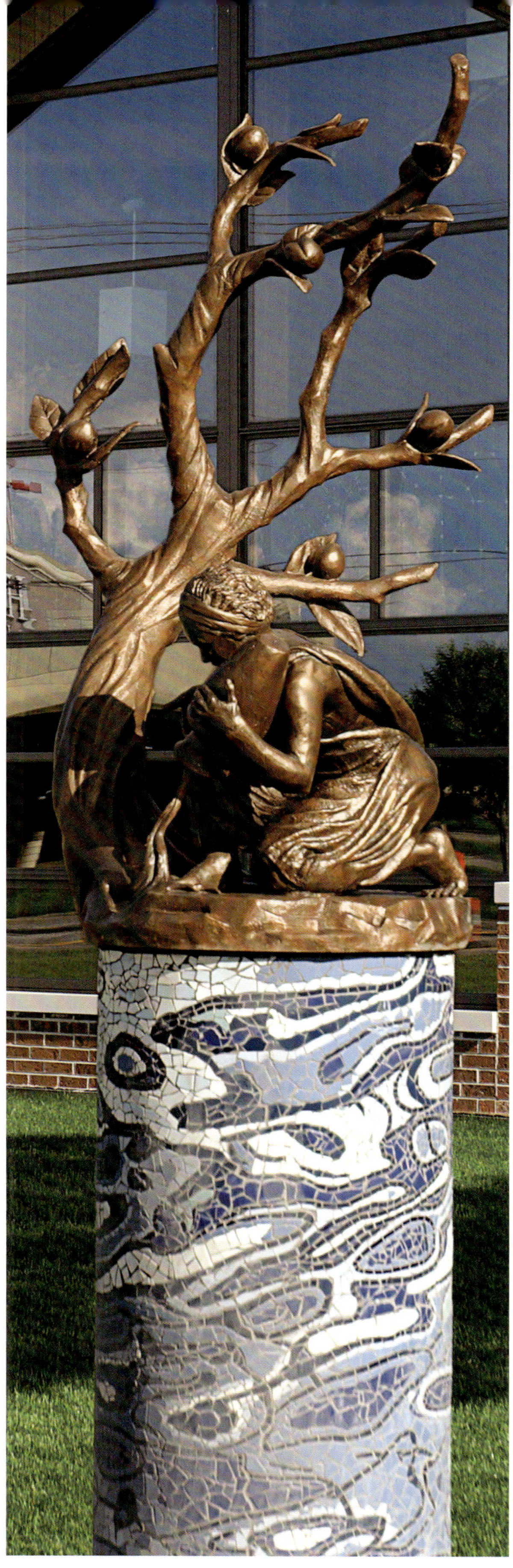

Ebb and Flow

SCULPTURE

LEAD ARTIST
Kathleen Scarboro

ASSISTANT ARTIST
Sarah Furst

MOSAIC

LEAD ARTIST
Sharka Glet

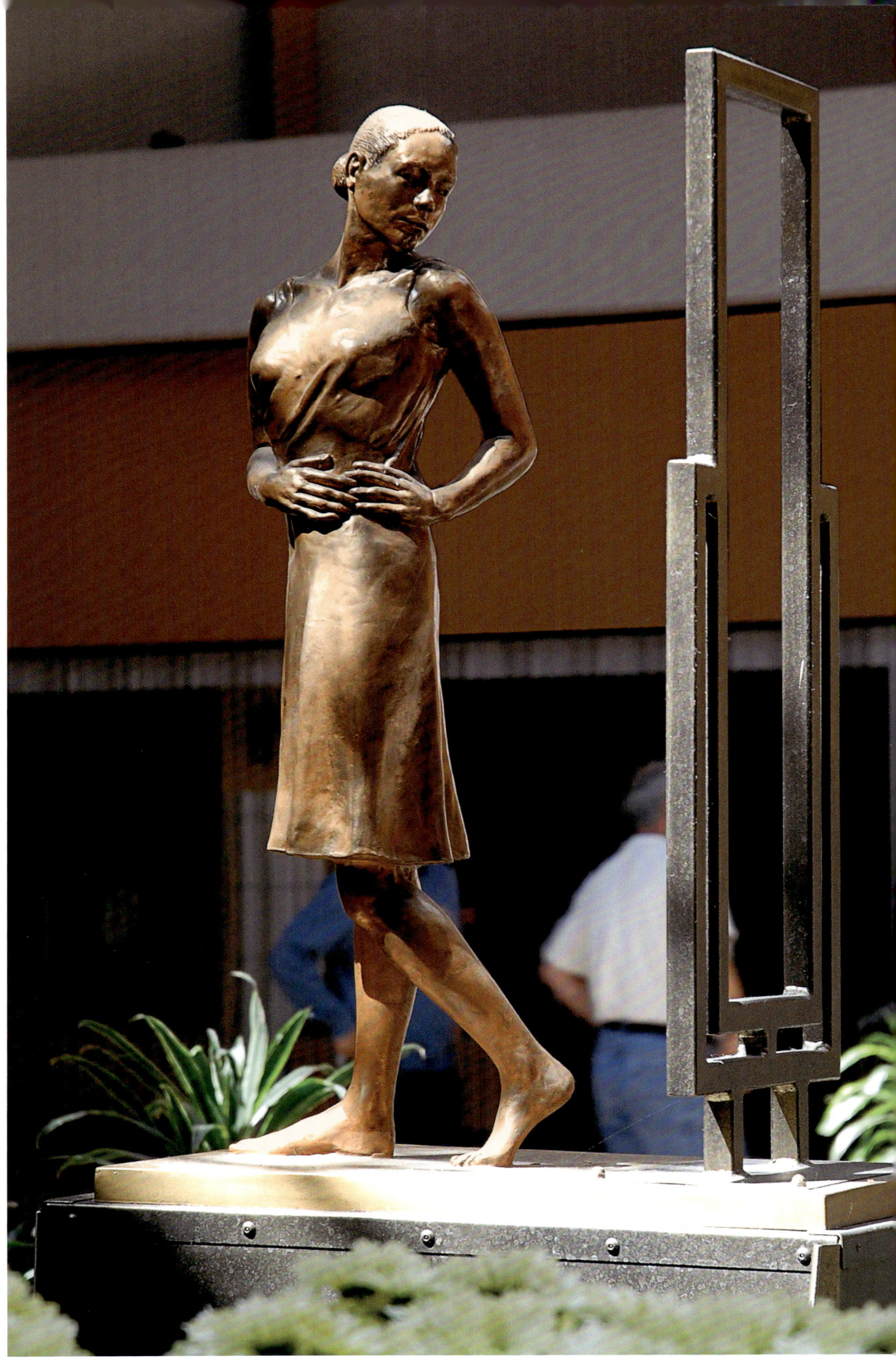

The New Dress

SCULPTURE	FABRICATED STEEL BASE
LEAD ARTIST	LEAD ARTIST
Kathleen Scarboro	**Marsha Lega**

The New Dress

Does the image speak
or hold her breath
when she hears the sharp-
edged mirrored truth?

Does the image turn
to glimpse or stare
at the surprised
elegance of the just-enough swing
of the summer Pima cotton crisp?

I think the image
strains to see all angles
places hidden only from self

Surely, the image must smile
at the recognition
of forgotten beauty and that this moment
is hers to keep.

GWENDOLYN MITCHELL

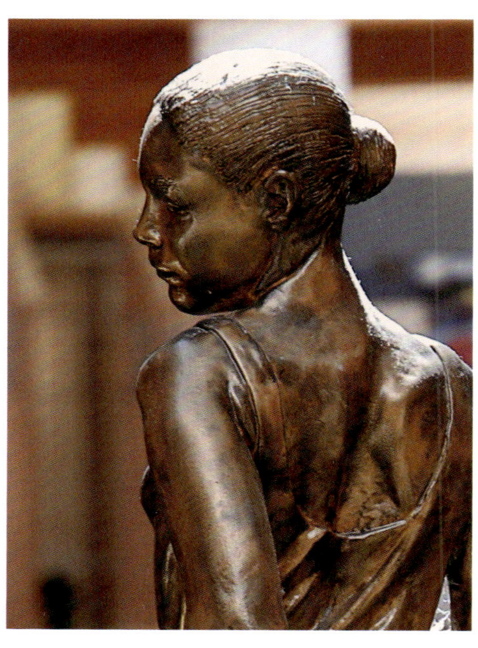

New Horn

Happy birthday, little man!
Put away your plastic flute
You are Gabriel now,
Golden as the sun.
That's what his mother would say.

He was a musical boy
Danced before he was born
She could feel him sometimes
While humming in the kitchen.

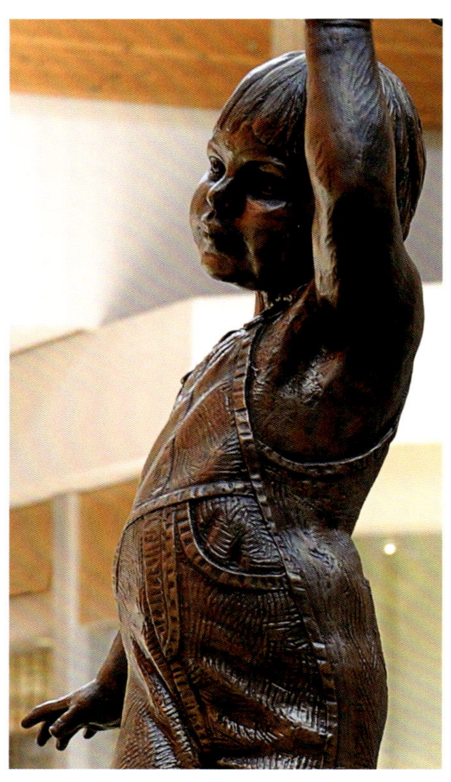

Wasn't but three
When he started finger-snapping
To radio tunes
Rode on his daddy's shoes
Those front porch summers
Learning to whistle and strum

He marched with the band at school
And played first chair.
Later did jazz solos
The likes of Miles Davis
His mother would say.

Dance bands came next
And concerts in the park
Later yet he played Taps
For a fallen friend.

Sorrowful sighs are remembered
And too many goodbyes
Came blowing from that horn
But it was the music that set him straight
And the music never strayed from his heart.
That's what his mother would say.

NANCY LOCKHART

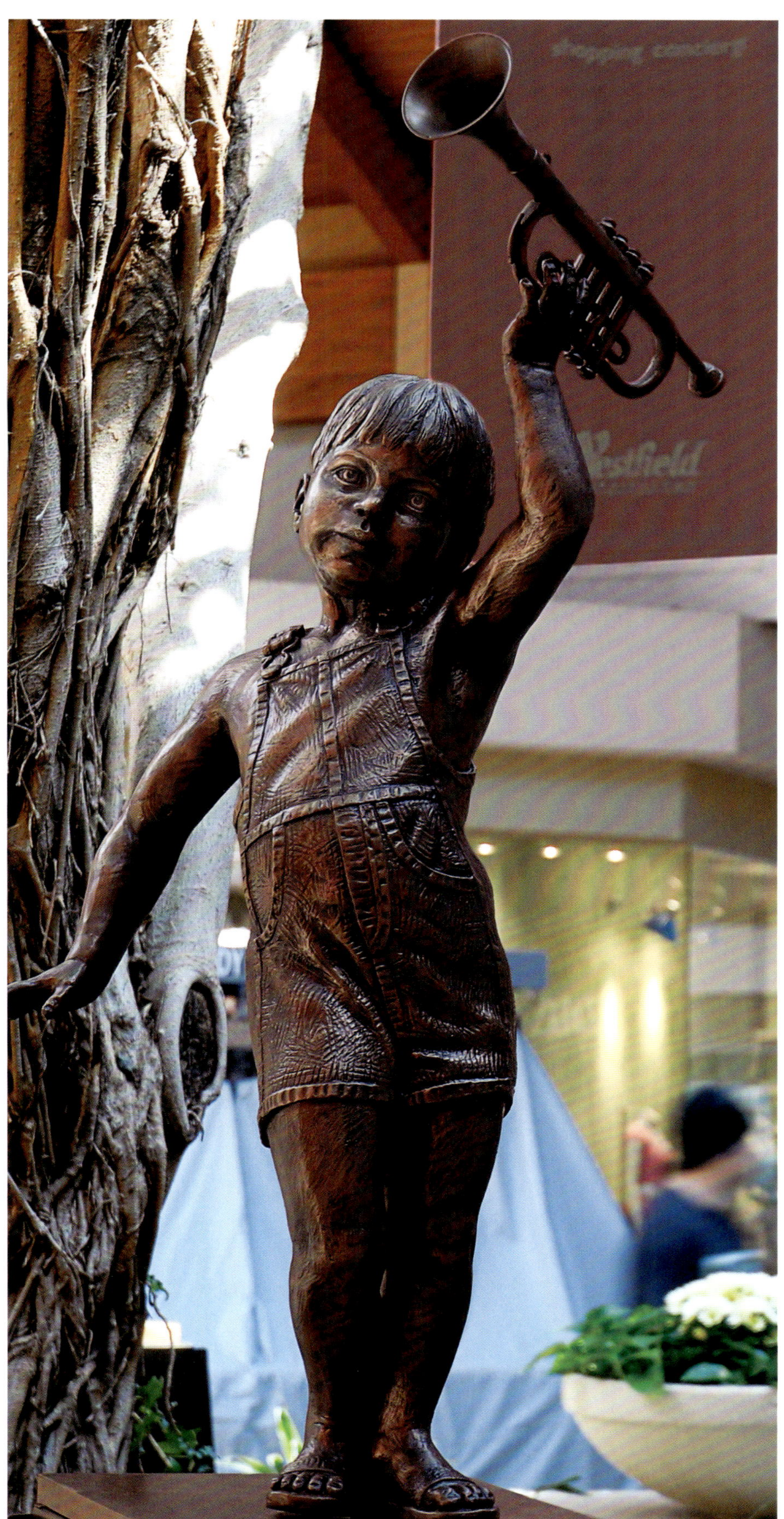

The Gift of Music

SCULPTURE

LEAD ARTIST

Kathleen Farrell

ASSISTANT ARTISTS

Sarah Furst,
Dante DiBartolo

FABRICATED STEEL BASE

LEAD ARTIST

Marsha Lega

I Wonder

Today I quit my book
To take a look around.
The clouds puffed up like words
With the sky like pages.

Chapter One was the sun
Before the thunder rages
My story was full of atmosphere
The characters rounded and weathered
My imagination was soaring
Like a party balloon untethered!

When my story's last page was turned
The stars and the moon did shine
And I was sure I'd never forget
The wonder that was mine

NANCY LOCKHART

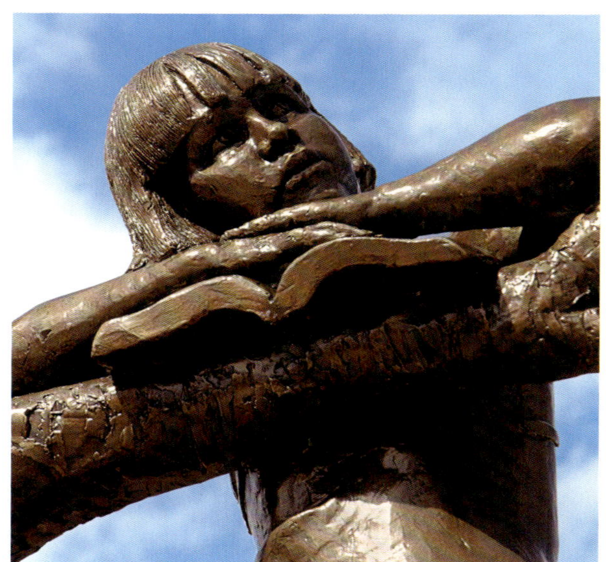

education

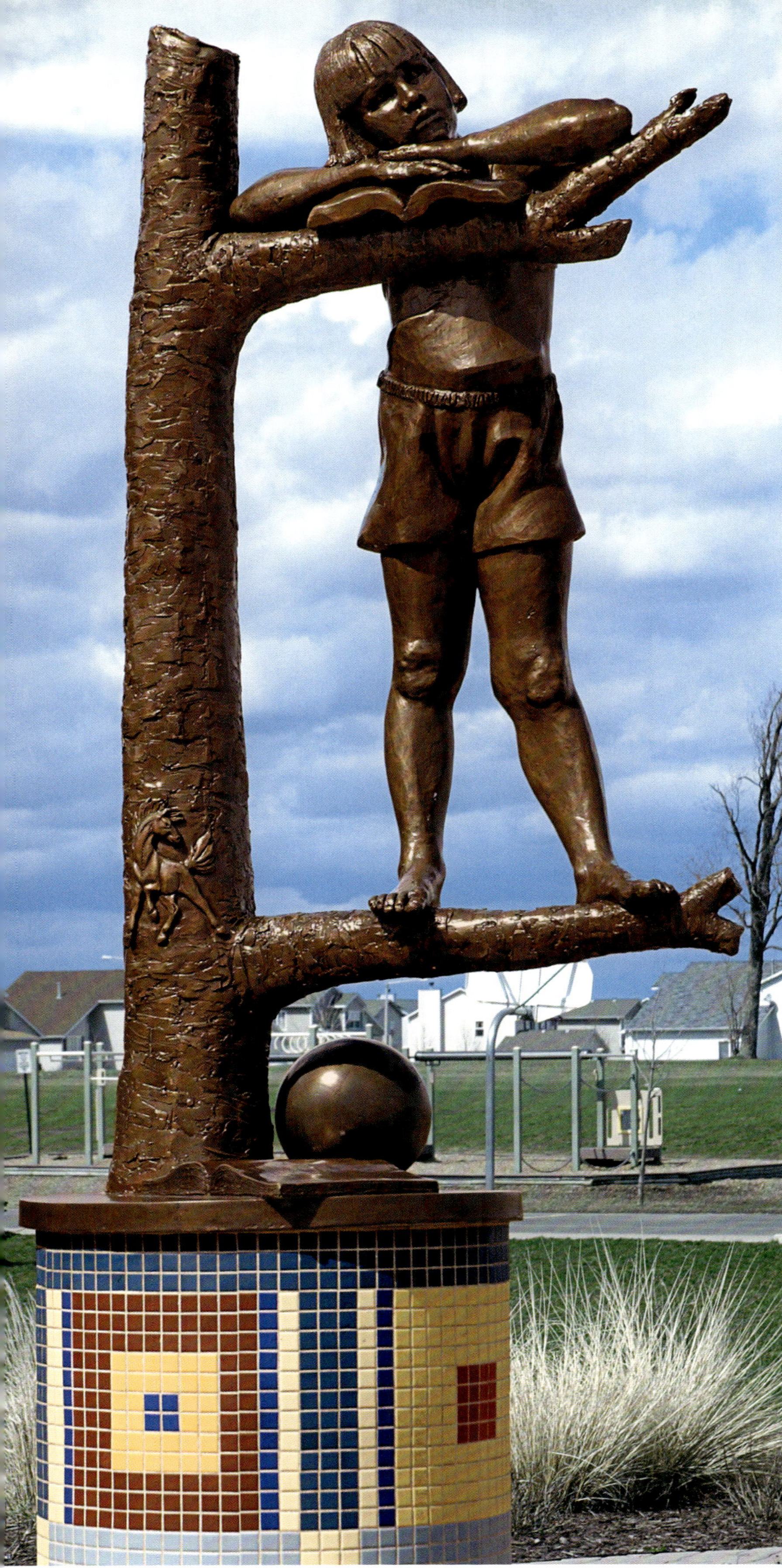

I Wonder (Meadowview Elementary School)

SCULPTURE

LEAD ARTIST
Kathleen Scarboro

MOSAIC

SIMPLE MOSAIC

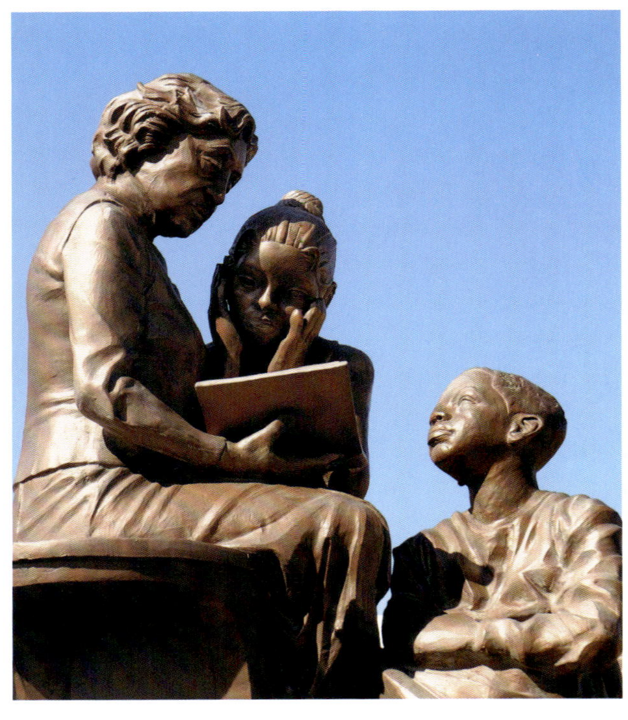

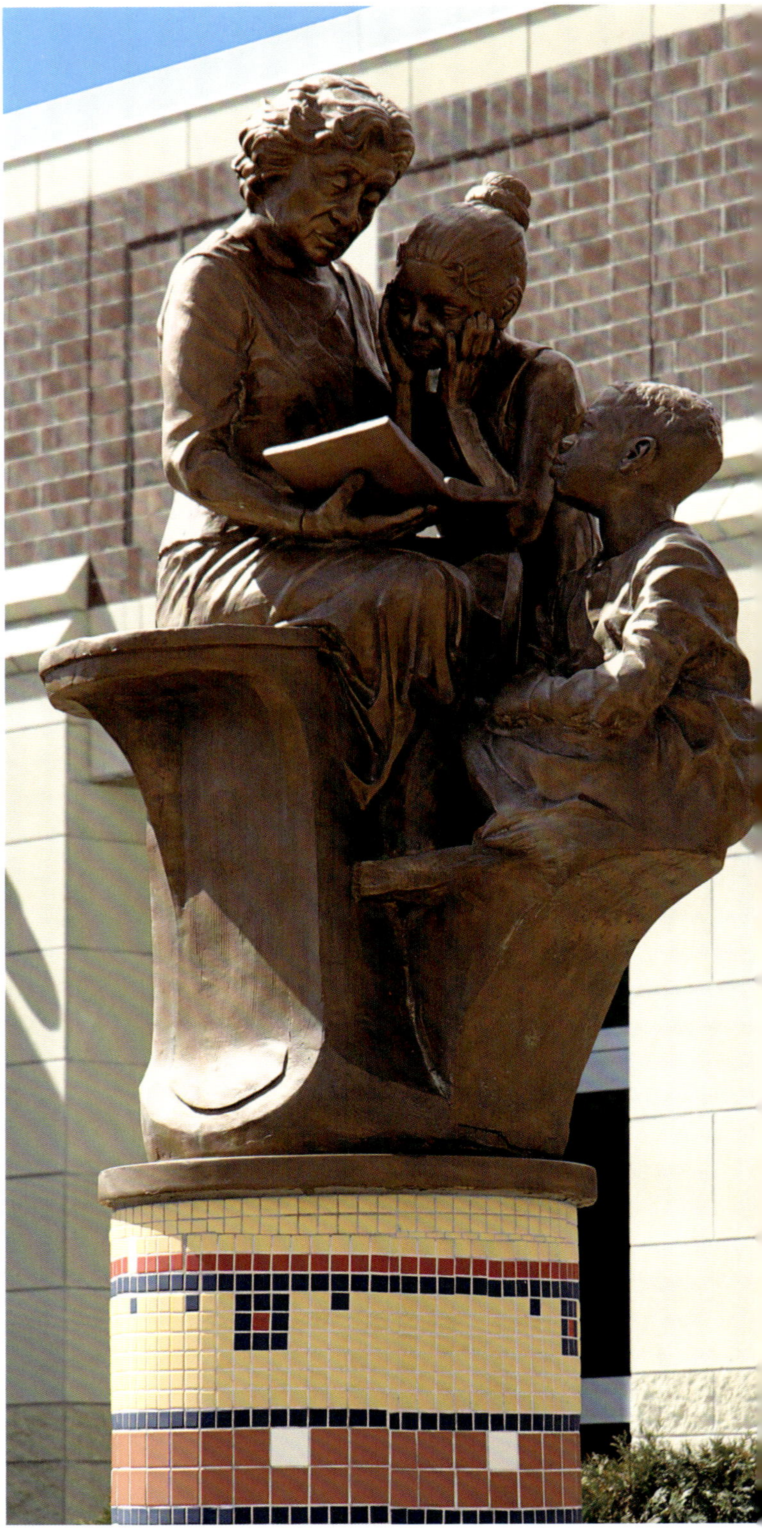

A Teacher's Gift (Sator Sanchez Elementary School)

SCULPTURE

LEAD ARTIST
Jesus Rodriguez

MOSAIC

SIMPLE MOSAIC

35

Bombardier Martyrdom

The USA named a B17 "Sator Sanchez"
To honor a Joliet WARRIOR
He was posthumously awarded The Medal of Honor
Because he set a record for bomb runs in W.W.II
And later died in action, a martyr for FREEDOM

Later Joliet erected Sator Sanchez School
Composed mostly of brick, steel, and limestone,
Solid stuff!
Yet its curving, geometric contours proclaim:
"Here flies a spirit!"

At the entrance the students are greeted by a statue
Composed of three figures:

A mature, dignified lady teacher is reading
To a boy about six sitting at her feet listening.
While a girl about ten stands at her side,
Looking at the printed words on the page.

The three are very real but also magical:
They are sculpted together in a circle design,
The boy is enraptured, inspired by hearing
The adventures of a Sator or Aladdin or Tom Sawyer,
The girl sees letters becoming sounds
That become characters, facts, theories...

Maybe the school and the Statue combine
To suggest a sort of secular prayer
That neither scientists, nor artists, nor citizens
Desire Bombardier Martyrdom for future boys and girls.

JOHN STOBART

High Expectations

These
Soliloquists

Handsomely honed necks
Tilted back into
Sheaths of drum-tight flesh

Look up, out, and over
A morass of progress

The prophet head slightly cocked peeks into the future
The guru arches back to see the zenith of the sun at summer solstice
The Messiah palms the Good Book

Their lonely soliloquies may spin into dialogue
When they realize they share the same soul

The prophet waits for the time of vindication
The guru for the time of enlightenment
The messiah for the time of sacrifice

Their wisdom winces
Until they see
The same heaven

GEORGE DAVID MILLER

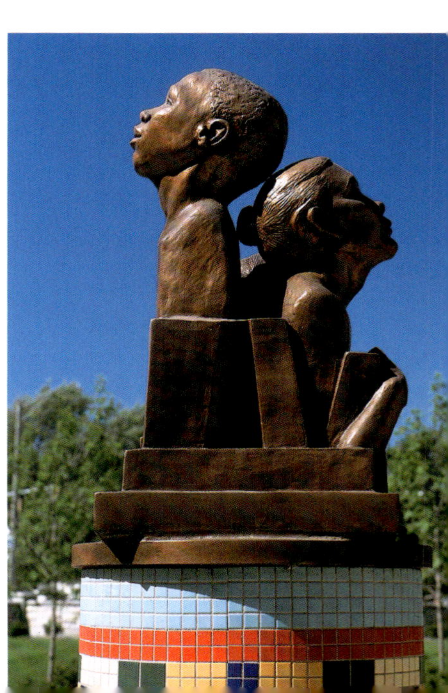

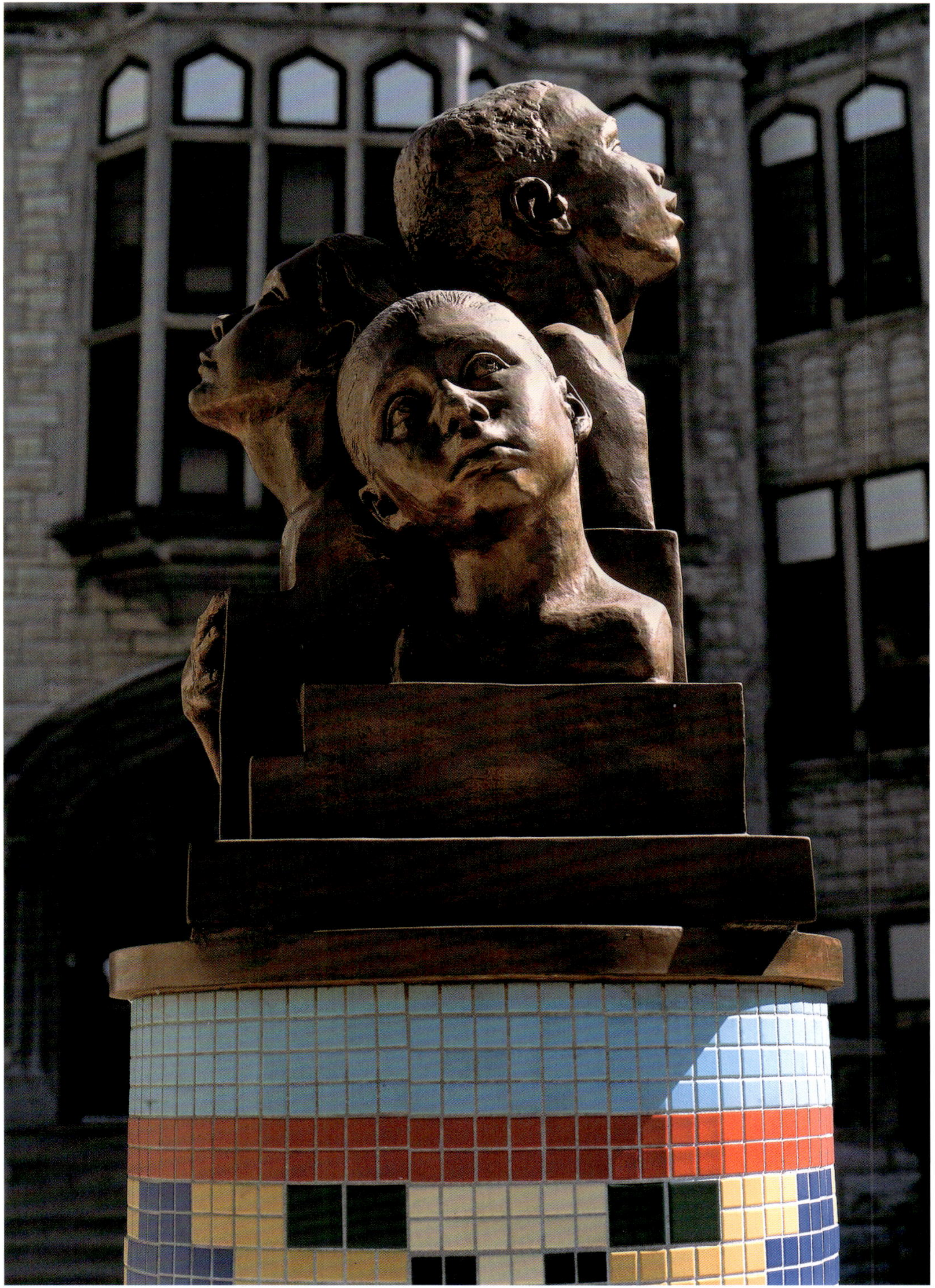

High Expectations (Washington Jr. High School)

SCULPTURE

LEAD ARTIST
Kathleen Scarboro

ASSISTANT ARTIST
Dante DiBartolo

MOSAIC

LEAD ARTIST
Kreshaun McKinney

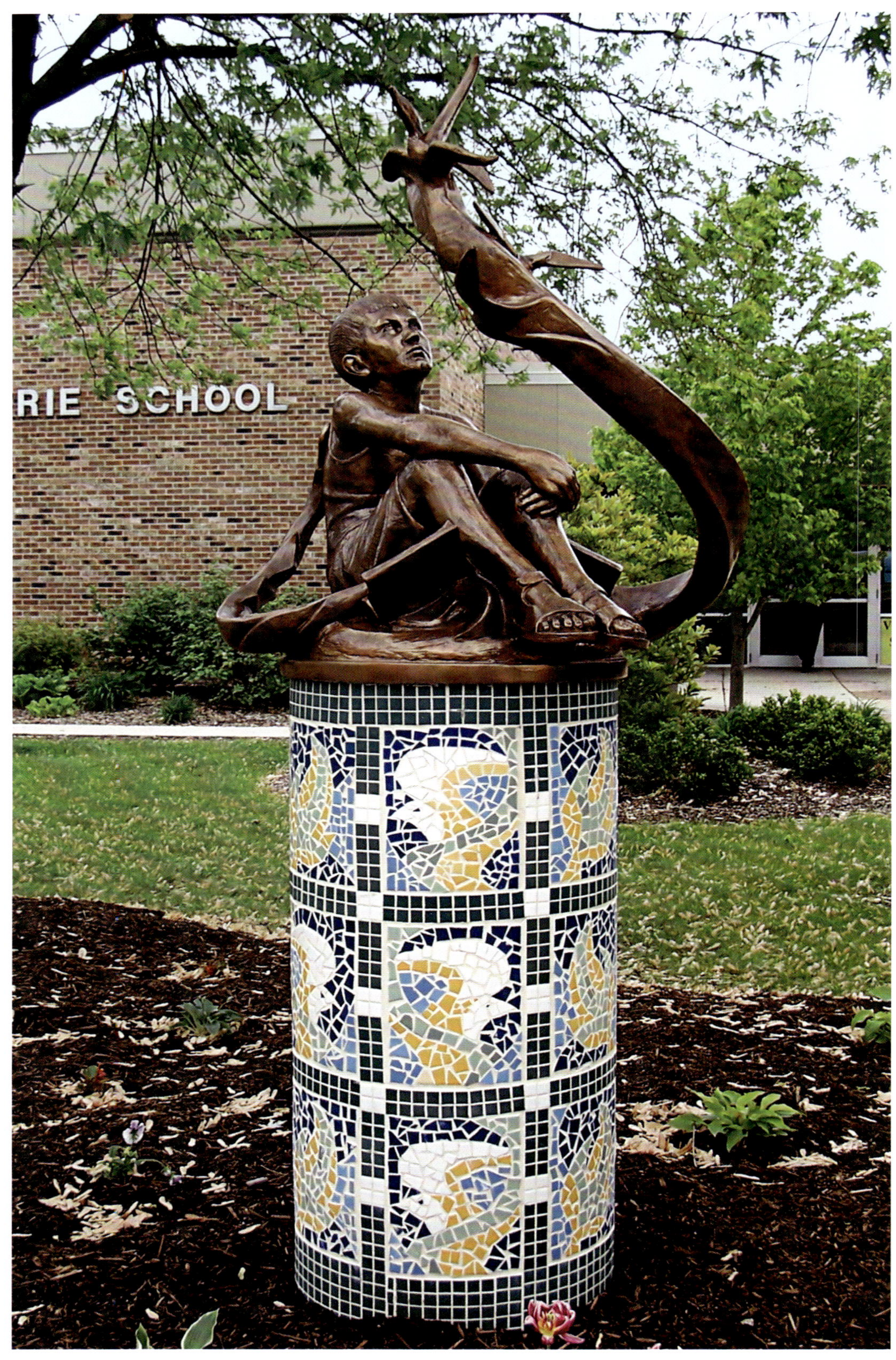

The Creative Spirit Soars (Grand Prairie Elementary School)

SCULPTURE	MOSAIC	
LEAD ARTIST **Sarah Furst**	LEAD ARTIST **Sarah Furst**	ASSISTANT ARTISTS **Grand Prairie students**

The Ponder Bird

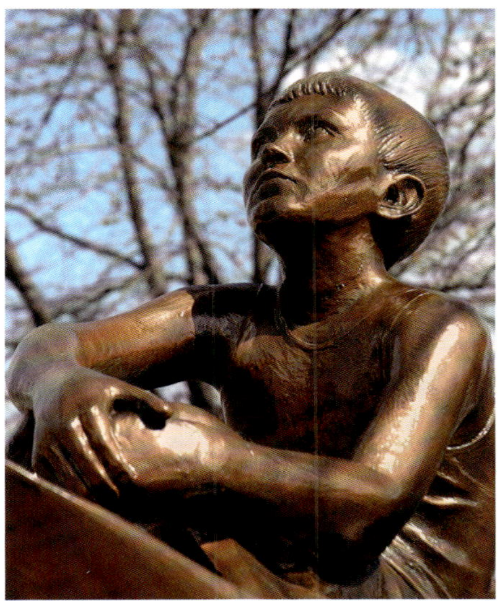

Old men can't see it.
Withered in the real,
Their eyes lose sight of the might be.
But reading boys can see it,
See the ponder bird as it circles
The carrion of lost civilizations,
Alighting to feed
On the carcasses of Caesars.
Or see it gliding to galaxies afar,
The frigate bird to rocket navies
Patrolling the gulfs between stars.
Or, flapping its exotic feathers,
Orbiting now over some orient opulence
Before diving into a paradox
Of poverty somewhere beyond the pale
Where pestilence and pathos interbreed.
And then, like a homing pigeon,
The ponder bird returns,
Roosting on the boy's head,
Like the raven on the bust of Pallas,
Where it will linger
'Til driven forcefully from its perch
By the whisper of turning pages.

TED THOMPSON

Reaching for our Destinies

Out of rock reason
Out of thinking truth
Out of reaching fantasy
Speculation
Heresy
And finally proof

Skin the sky with eyes
Pray for the next day
For the freedom
Of new bounty
Largesse only
Limited by
Minimalization
Marginalization
Or praying youth

Will droplets of wisdom
Slip through fingers
Or nestle in palms

GEORGE DAVID MILLER

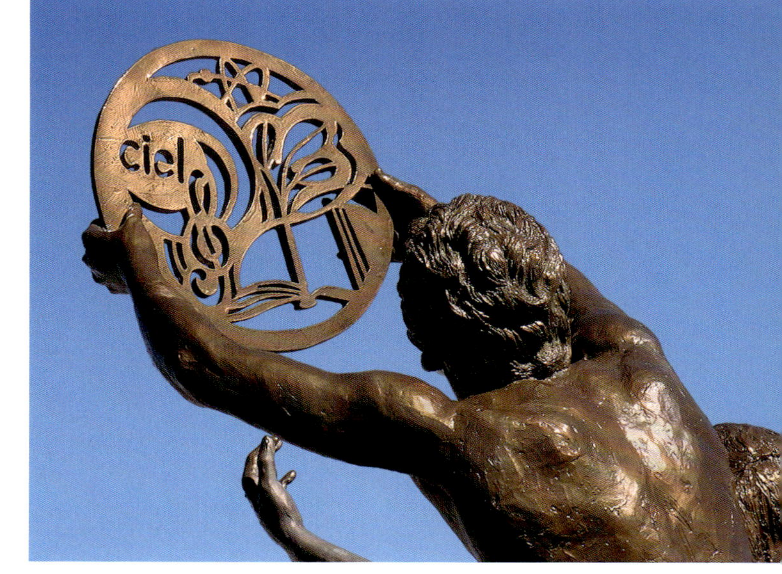

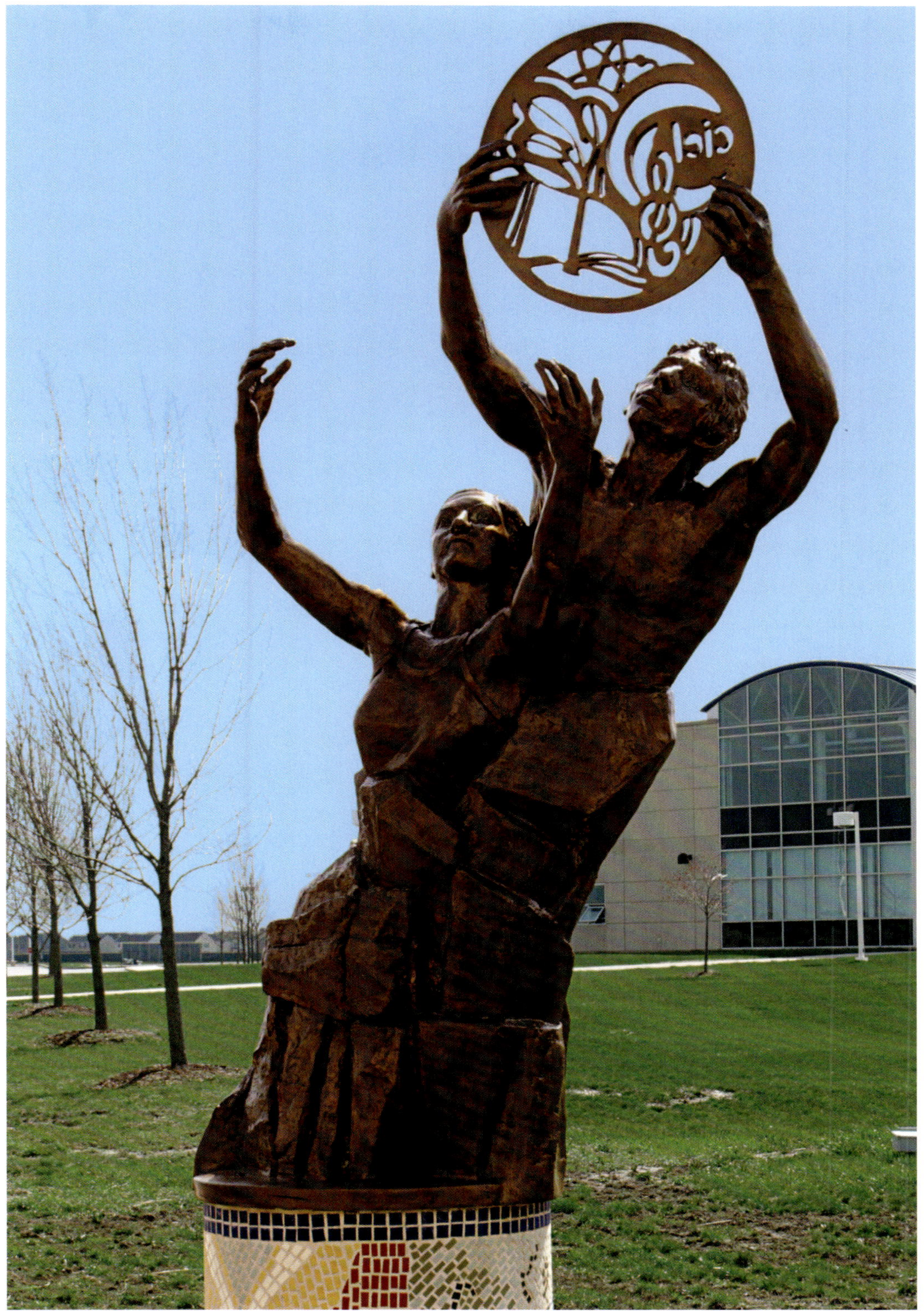

Reaching for Our Destinies (Plainfield South High School)

SCULPTURE

LEAD ARTIST
Kathleen Scarboro

ASSISTANT ARTIST
Dante DiBartolo

MOSAIC

LEAD ARTIST
Denise Reyes-Albright

ASSISTANT ARTIST
Plainfield South High School art students

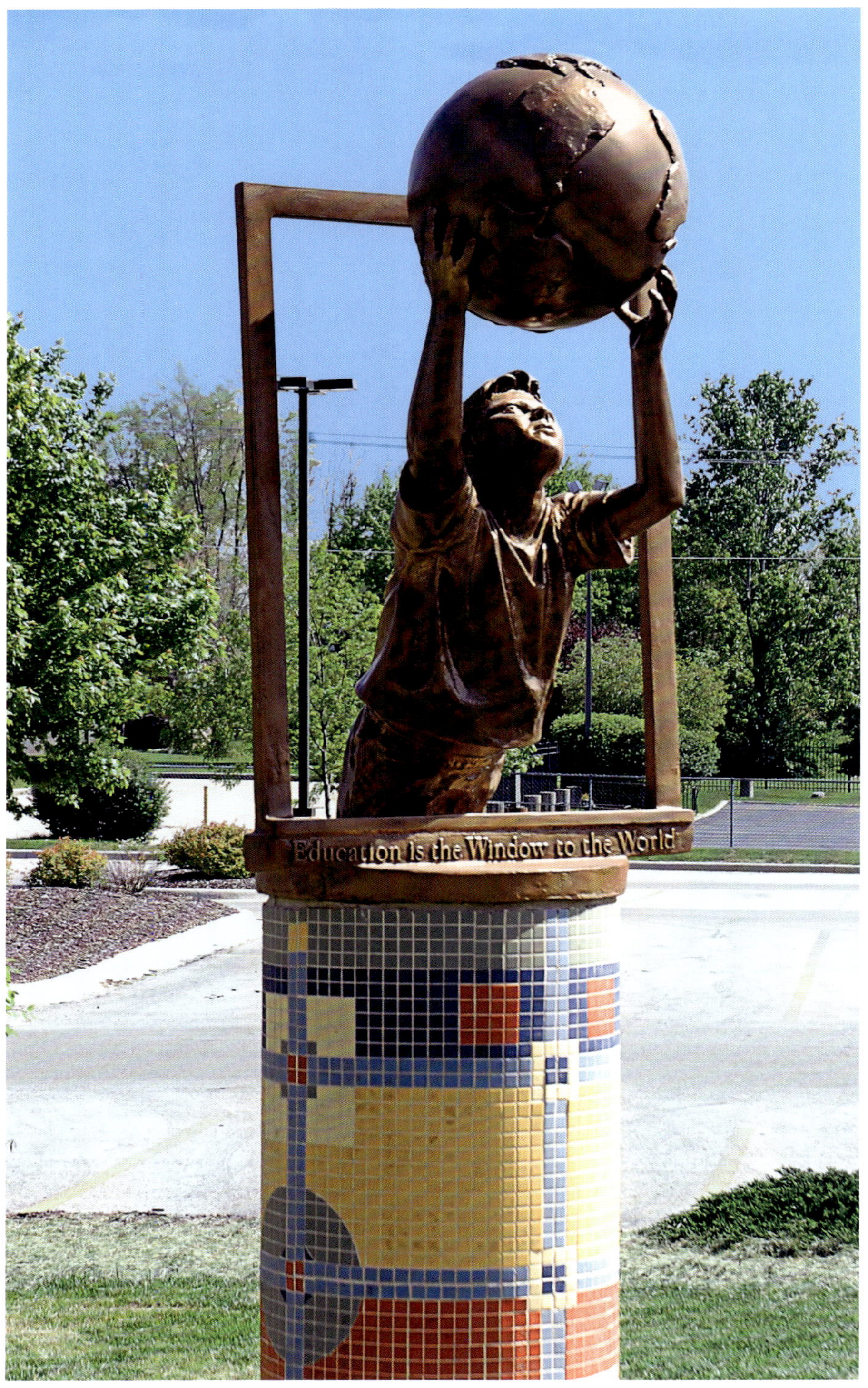

Education is the Window to the World (Dirksen Jr. High School)

SCULPTURE

LEAD ARTISTS
Sharka Glet,
Kelly Yadura-Gallaher

MOSAIC

LEAD ARTIST
Kelly Yadura-Gallaher

March Madness: Intergalactic League

Pondering this sleek, Atlas-like modern youth
Reaching high through an opportune window at school
To rebound the round ball called Earth—
I say to my companion, a righteous type fan,
    "Hoss, you know, that Chicken Little in the story,
    He ought to get more respect. Like this dude,
    That little chickee was up to saving our butts."
But Mr. Realistic is disdainful,
    "That Cornish Hen is dumb as dirt.
    The sky can't fall at all, at all!
    That's as dumb as blaming Acid Rain
    On power plants' burning coal
    Or the Greenhouse Effect on hairsprays and auto exhausts."
So I match his disdain, and trump his ignorance:
    "Well, listen up, Mister. I'll bet you don't know
    that right now Soviet and American missiles armed
    with nuclear warheads can be launched in five
    minutes at every population center in the
    Western Hemisphere with 25,000 people or more.
    And that 14 nuclear power plants in Northern
    Illinois alone could detonate enough now inert
    Radioactive fuel and waste to make the 2004
    Tsunami seem a tempest in a teacup.*
    For the sky to fall might be more humane."
Then he trembled and panted but spoke fervently
    "Yea then would be the end
    But all the enraptured would be led to Heaven,
    Leaving Earth to Satan!"
And I groaned and hoped for a Darwin or Einstein
To be well enough educated by school and life
To keep the sky from falling.

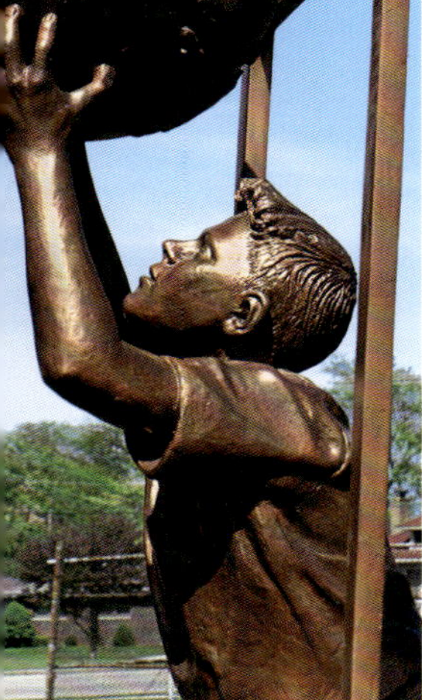

JOHN STOBART

*See Dr. Helen Goldicutt, The New Nuclear Danger

Child Guide

She arrives in a gown all green;
Flowers sewn in at every seam.
Her path is a river that's deep and gleams.
The children want to follow, it seems.

They ride her craft with a trust grown bold
And scale her hills, climb when told,
Seed to tree, book to gift, they evolve, unfold.
Unique, wisdom winks, "Children do not always mold."

She washes them in art, dresses their hair in song.
Thoughts and words embrace to challenge the throng.
The lucky, the free, dance brave and belong.
Feet are led, path is fed for those who go along.

She comes to teach, stays to reach, emerald her gown.
She nurtures mind and spirit. In fertile ground, being is found.

KIM VOLLMER-LAWSON

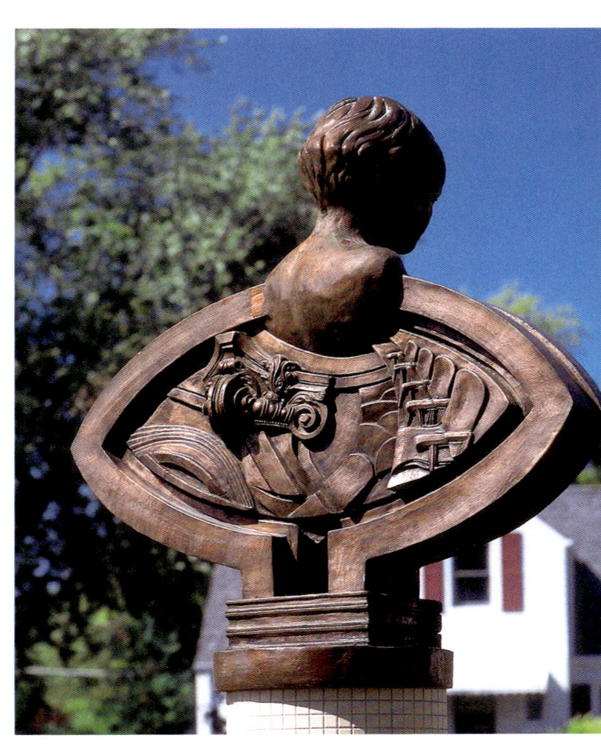

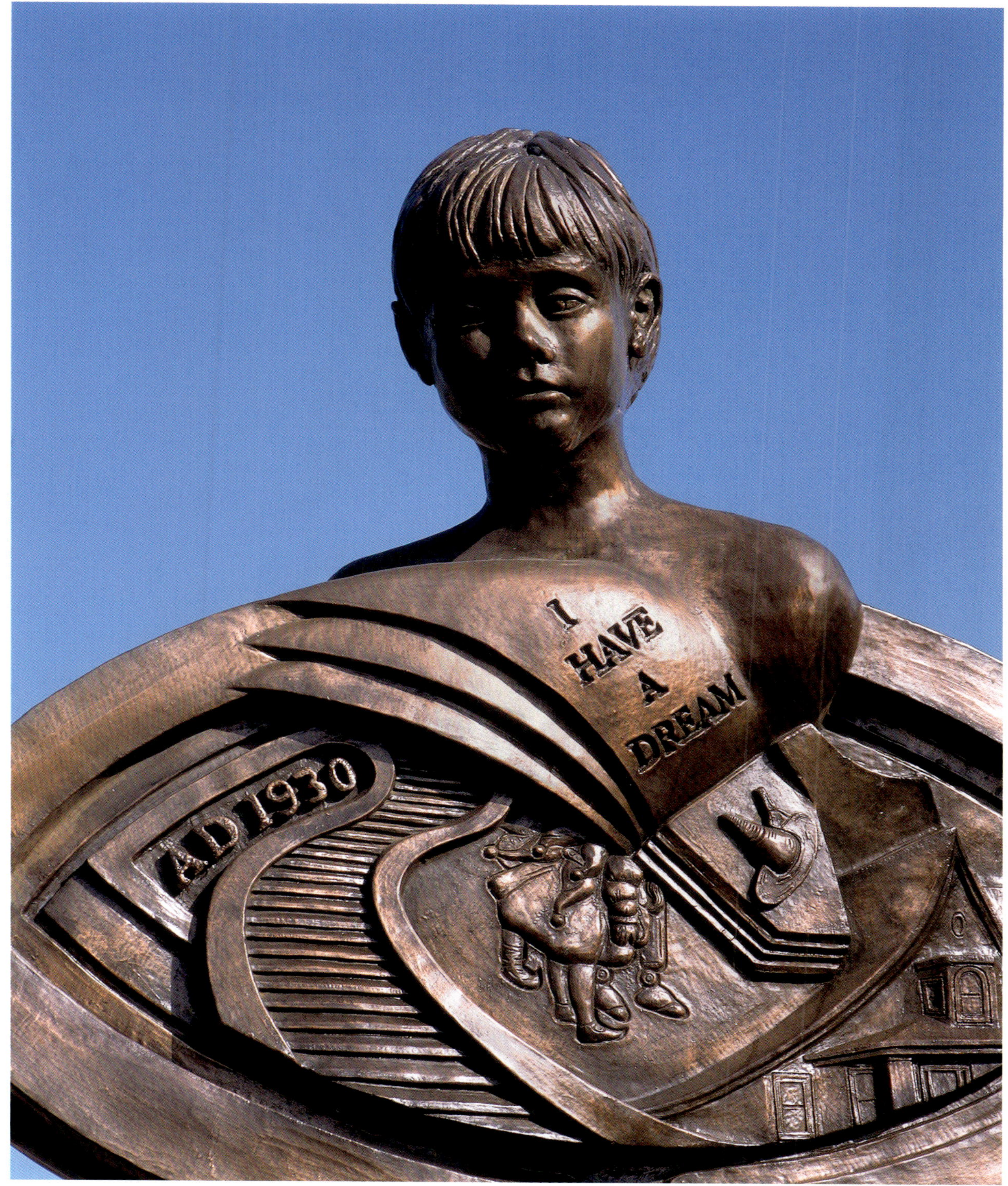

Planting the Seeds: Children and Education (Taft Elementary School)

SCULPTURE

LEAD ARTIST
Kathleen Scarboro

ASSISTANT ARTIST
Dante DiBartolo

MOSAIC

SIMPLE MOSAIC

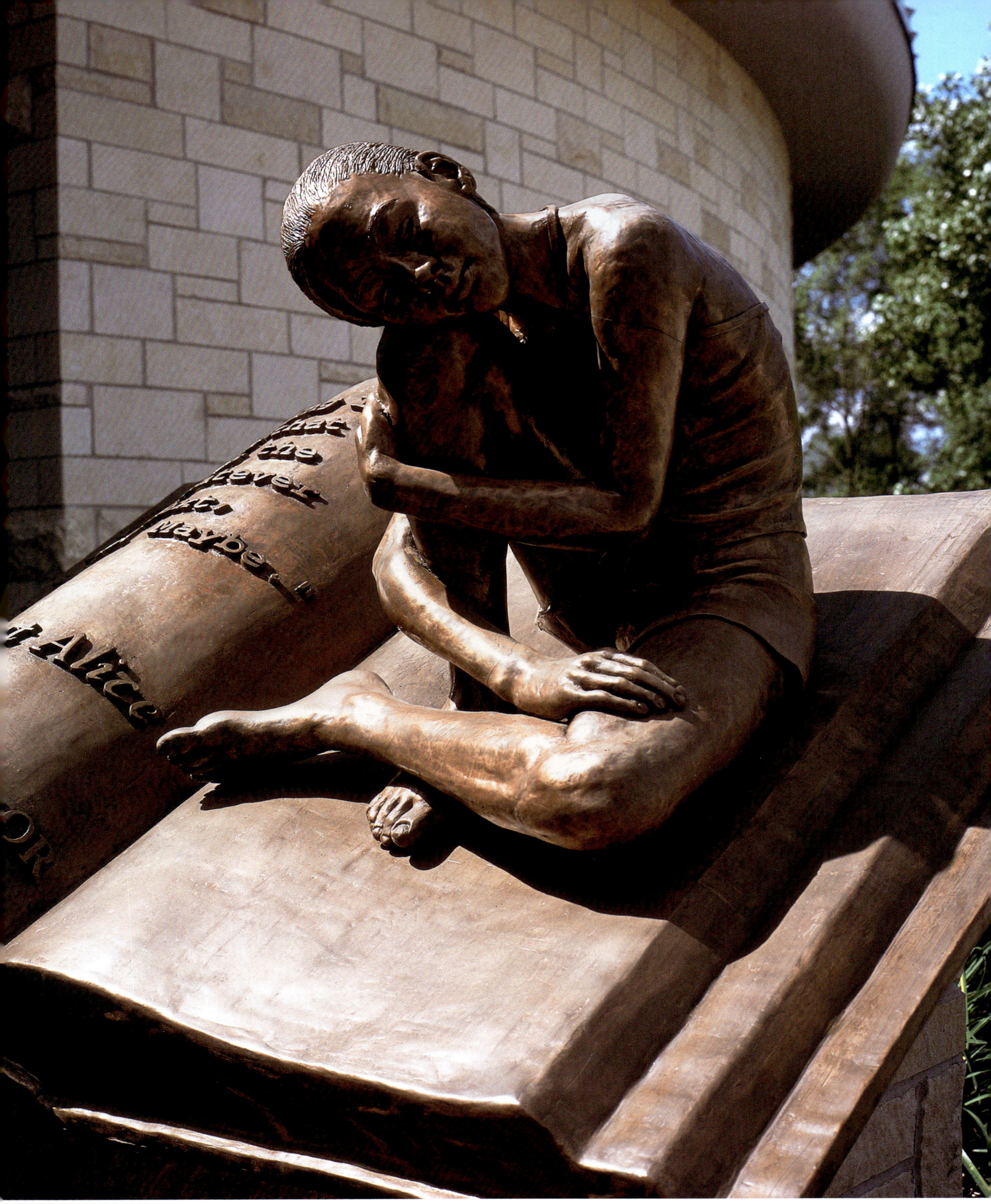

Alice: Phyllis Reynolds Naylor's Young Heroine

SCULPTURE

LEAD ARTIST
Kathleen Scarboro

ASSISTANT ARTISTS
Dante DiBartolo, Roger Carlson

Alice on a Book

While perched on ALL ABOUT ALICE in brass,
Pretending calm and happy time "cool,"
Superheroine Al appears nobody's fool
All posed a la guru in a lotus with "sass."
She's Naylor's motherless modern lass
Adrift in schemes and plots to rule
Her father and brother and kids at school,
While feeling great guilt and wanting more "class."
There remains a rascal in Al's angelic poses,
A tiny devil peeps out from her roses
As she blooms from 10 to infinite in Alice books.
The artist sculpts Alice's elfin looks.
The text tells the sardonic behind her face,
Happy-sad charmer with substance and grace.

"The only thing I knew for sure was that nothing
stays the same, and whatever was coming next,
I'd be ready. Maybe…"*

JOHN STOBART

*This quotation was selected by Phyllis Reynolds Naylor (the author of the Alice novels and a former Jolietan) to suggest the essence of Alice in a few words in an interview by the sculptor, Kathleen Scarboro.

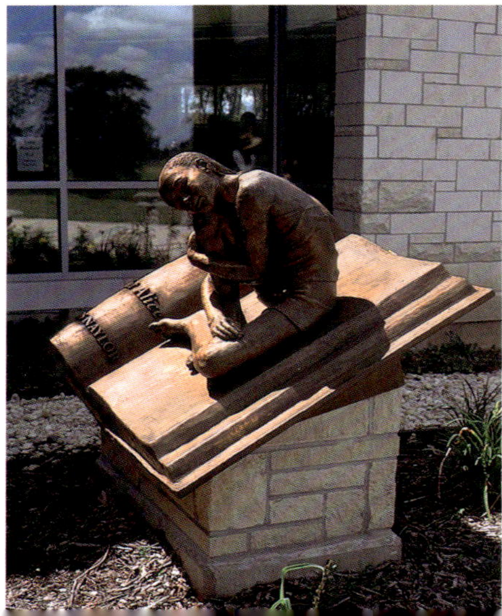

Artists

LEAD SCULPTORS

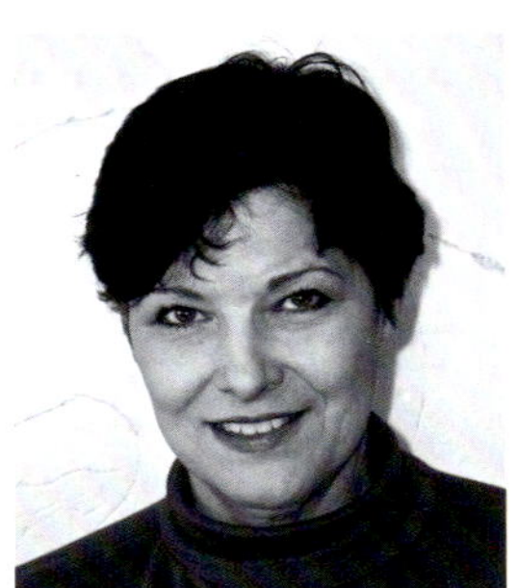

NAME Farrell, Kathleen

BORN Chicago, IL

EDUCATION/EXPERIENCE Master of Fine Arts, Printmaking, L' École Nationale Supérieure des Arts Décoratifs, French Ministry of Culture, Paris France (1978); Master of Arts, Cultural Anthropology, Governors State University (1975); Bachelor of Arts, Painting, Southern Illinois University (1971)

CURRENT STATUS Studio painter, sculptor, and mosaicist specializing in art for labor unions, FCPA artist and President. She currently resides in Joliet, Illinois.

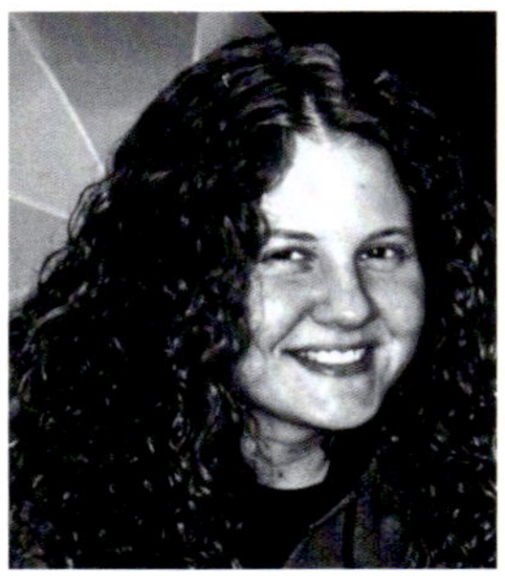

NAME Furst, Sarah

BORN Midland, MI

EDUCATION/EXPERIENCE Bachelor of Fine Arts with emphasis in sculpture, the School of the Art Institute of Chicago (2001)

CURRENT STATUS Sculptor, mosaicist, studio painter, and FCPA artist. She currently resides in Chicago and works in Joliet, Illinois.

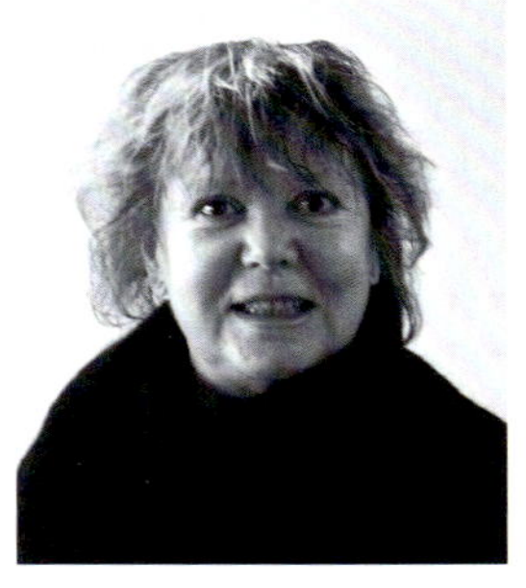

NAME Glet, Sharka Marie Frantiska

BORN Prague, Czech Republic

EDUCATION/EXPERIENCE Master of Arts, Book Illustration, Charles University of Art, Prague, Czech Republic (1968); Bachelor of Arts, Art with concentration in sculpture, decorative, graphic, and fine art, Academy of Arts, Czech Republic (1962).

CURRENT STATUS FCPA mural painter, FCPA lead mosaicist and sculptor in Joliet, Illinois. Freelance book cover designer, illustrator, and fine artist. Sharka currently resides in Joliet with her husband.

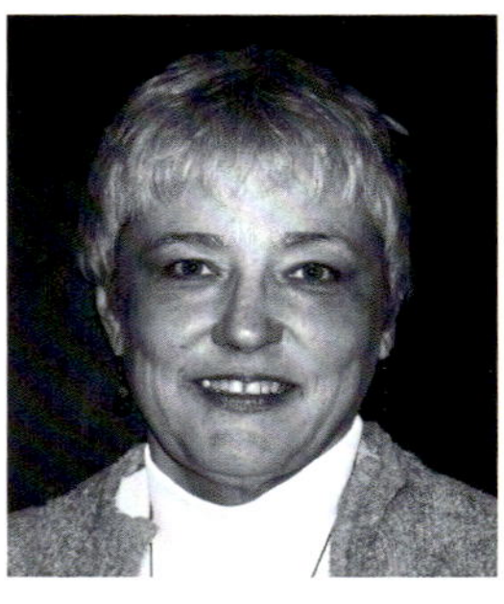

NAME Lega, Marsha

BORN Chicago, IL

EDUCATION/EXPERIENCE Master of Arts, Sculpture, Governors State University (1976); Bachelor of Arts, Art, the College of St. Francis (1967).

CURRENT STATUS Metal sculptor and furniture designer. Marsha currently resides in Joliet with her husband.

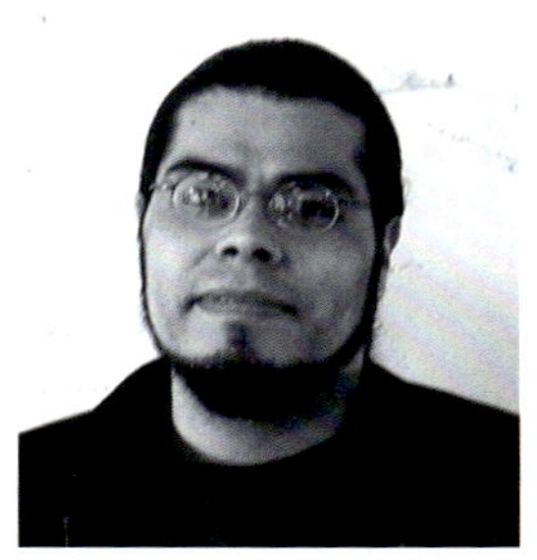

NAME Rodriguez, Jesus

BORN Morelia, Michoacan, Mexico

EDUCATION/EXPERIENCE Associate in Arts and Science, Fine Art, American Academy of Art.(1994)

CURRENT STATUS Master Tattoo Artist, FCPA painter, muralist, and mosaicist. Jesus currently resides in Joliet, Illinois.

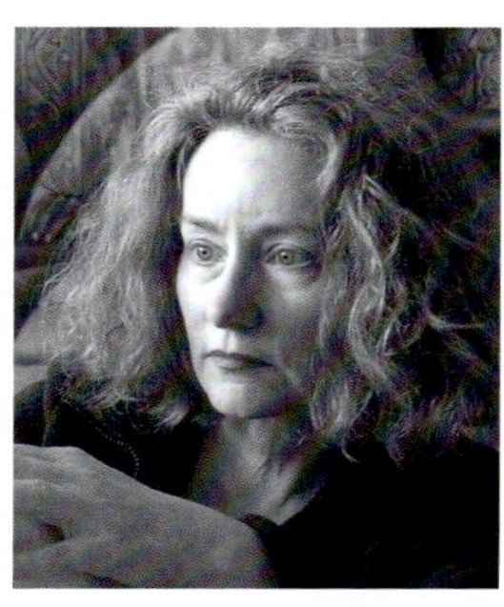

NAME Scarboro, Kathleen

BORN Chicago, IL

EDUCATION/EXPERIENCE Master of Fine Arts, Printmaking, École des Beaux Arts, Paris, France (1978); Bachelor of Arts, Painting, Southern Illinois University (1974) collaborating with Kathleen Farrell since 1977.

CURRENT STATUS Studio artist specializing in painting daily life in India, FCPA muralist, mosaicist, and sculptor. Kathleen divides time between studios in Joliet and Paris, France.

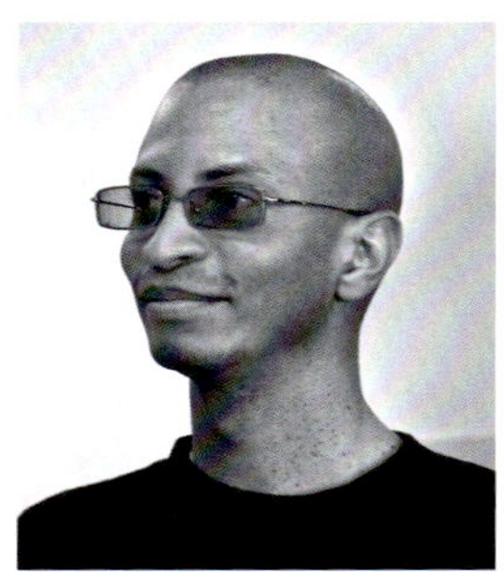

NAME Standifer, David

BORN Albany, GA

EDUCATION/EXPERIENCE Master of Fine Arts, Sculpture, the School of the Art Institute of Chicago (1994); Bachelor of Arts, Sculpture and Painting, the School of the Art Institute of Chicago (1992); Instructor of Sculpture and Figure Sculpture at the School of the Art Institute of Chicago (1995–2004).

CURRENT STATUS Studio artist specializing in sculpture and figurative sculptor. Currently, David resides in Chicago, Illinois.

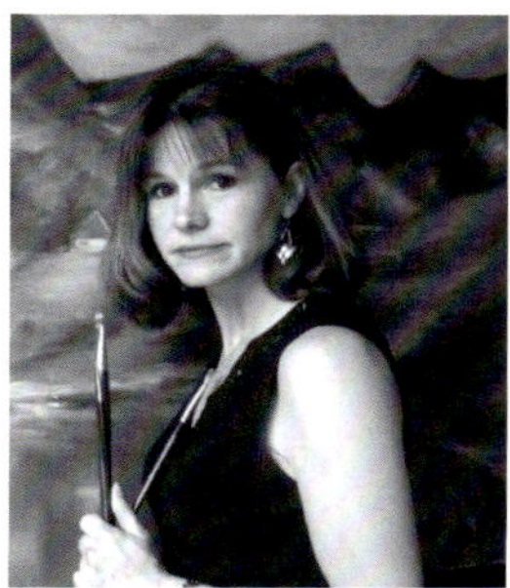

NAME Yadura-Gallaher, Kelly

BORN Joliet, IL

EDUCATION/EXPERIENCE Bachelor of Arts in Art with emphasis in biology, Northern Illinois University (1985); Medical Illustrator/photographer, St. Francis Hospital (1986); FCPA Muralist.

CURRENT STATUS Studio artist specializing in lustrous Technique Mixte, watercolorist and for the past seven years taught watercolor and Technique Mixte classes. Kelly currently resides in Austin, TX with her husband and four children and she is working on a new book that showcases artists in their studio spaces.

ARMATURE MAKER

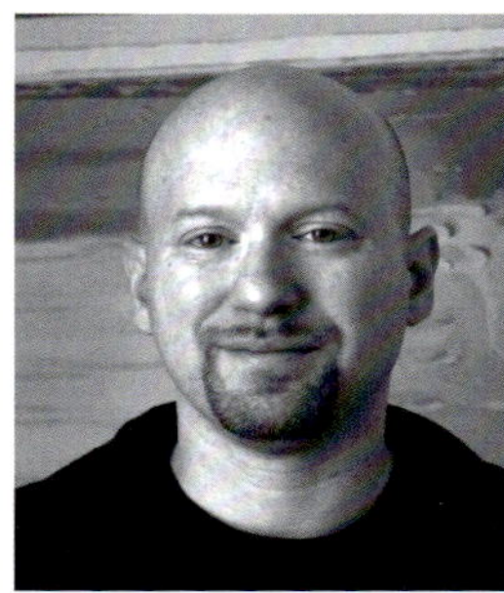

NAME DiBartolo, Dante

BORN Burbank, IL

EDUCATION/EXPERIENCE Associate of Arts, Joliet Junior College (1993); apprenticed with FCPA (1995–1998); trained as a sculptor, Visions Display Shop, Coal City, IL (1994–1998)

CURRENT STATUS FCPA sculptor, FCPA lead mosaicist and mural painter. Dante lives in Elwood, Illinois.

LEAD MOSAICIST

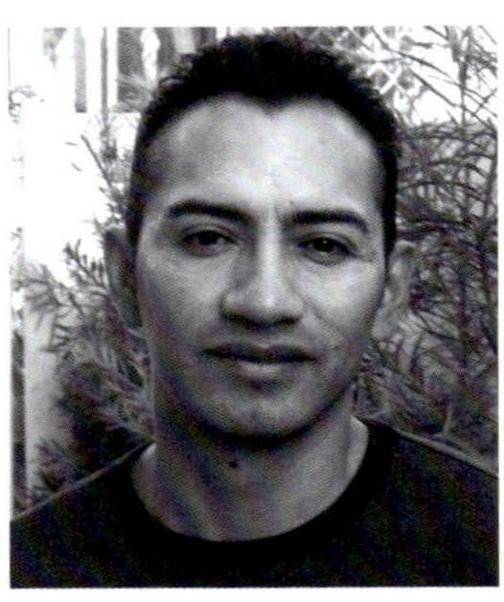

NAME Chavira, Saul

BORN Villa Juarez, San Luis Potosi, Mexico

EDUCATION/EXPERIENCE Undergraduate studies in Art, Joliet Junior College, undergraduate studies in Art and Architecture, University of New Mexico..

CURRENT STATUS FCPA artist specializing in mosaic and sculpture. Saul grew up in Joliet, Illinois.

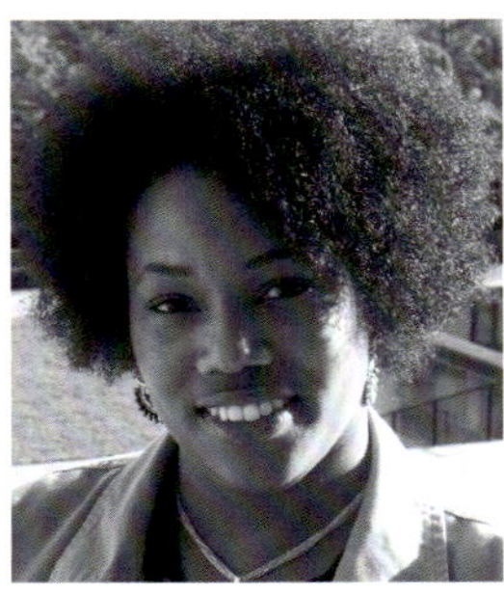

NAME McKinney, Kreshaun

BORN Harvey, IL

EDUCATION/EXPERIENCE Master of Fine Arts, Painting, Tyler School of Art (1997); Bachelor of Fine Arts, the School of the Art Institute of Chicago (1994); undergraduate and graduate studies at Temple University Rome, Rome Italy, (1993–94, 1996).

CURRENT STATUS Studio Programs teacher at the Nelson-Atkins Museum of Art, Kansas City, MO, where Kreshaun currently resides.

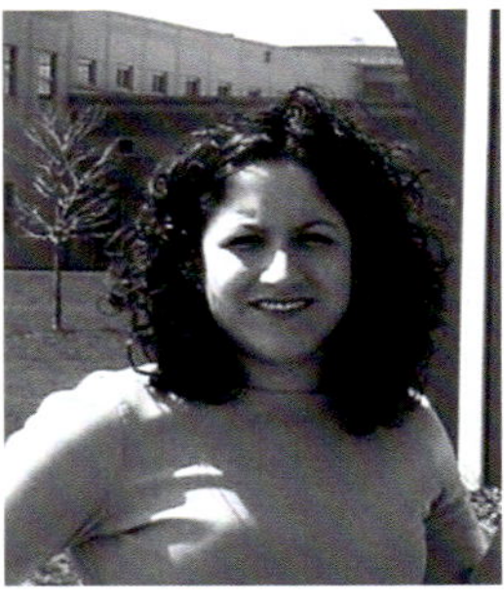

NAME Reyes-Albright, Denise

BORN Chicago, IL

EDUCATION/EXPERIENCE Master of Science, Art Education, Northern Illinois University, DeKalb (2003); Bachelor of Science, Art Education, Northern Illinois University (1993); FCPA Mural Training (2000).

CURRENT STATUS Art Teacher at Plainfield South High School, Plainfield, IL. Also devotes time to drawing and portrait commissions. Denise's students have been her creative outlet for many years. She enjoys working with FCPA as an artist and facilitator.

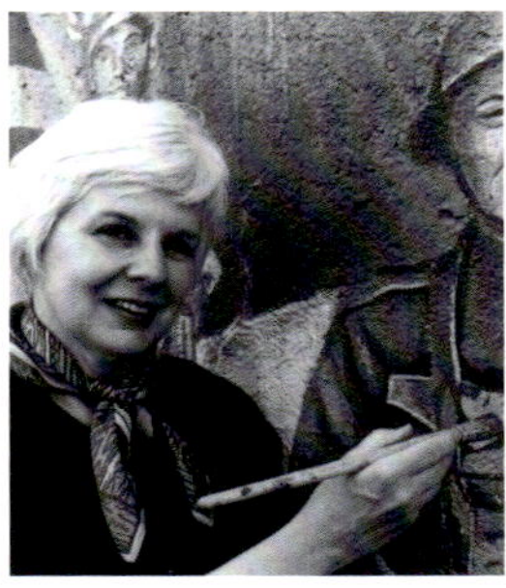

NAME Andrea Rountree

BORN Orangeburg, SC

EDUCATION/EXPERIENCE Master of Fine Arts, Painting, Northern Illinois University (1991); Master of Arts, Drawing, Northern Illinois University (1989); Bachelor of Arts, Art History, University of Georgia (1996)

CURRENT STATUS Studio painter and member of the Griffin Art group. Andrea currently resides in Savannah, GA.

Poets

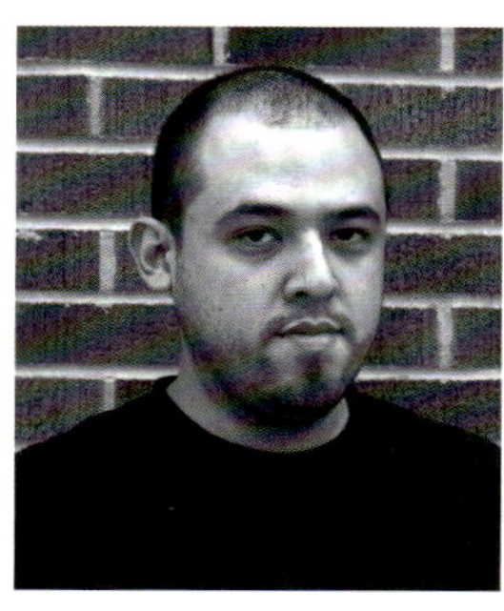

NAME Silva, Ilario

BORN Joliet, IL

EDUCATION/EXPERIENCE Completed studies at American Academy of Art.

CURRENT STATUS FCPA artist. Ilario resides in Joliet, Illinois.

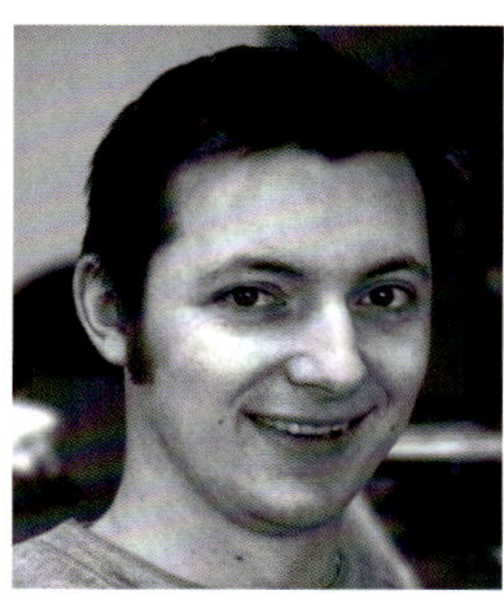

NAME Yanchick, David

BORN Joliet, IL

EDUCATION/EXPERIENCE Bachelor of Science, Game Art & Design, Westwood College (2006); Bachelor of Science, Art, concentration in Drawing, Olivet Nazarene University (2002); Associate of Arts, Art, Joliet Junior College (2000); studied Technique Mixte with Patrick Betaudier, 2002–03.

CURRENT STATUS Currently pursuing a career in video game art and design. David resides in Joliet with his wife.

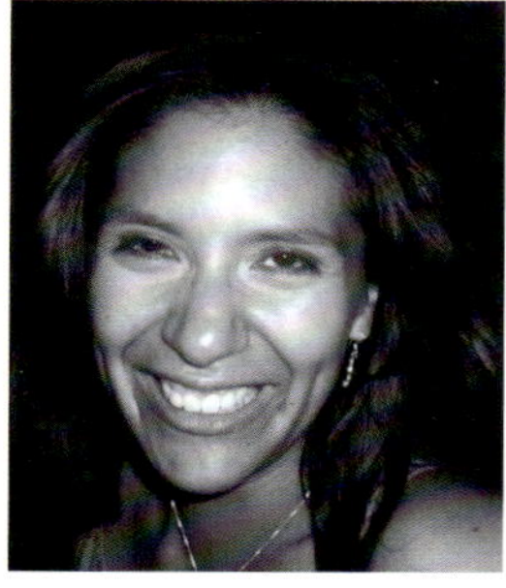

NAME Bardales, Katherrine

BORN Chicago, IL

EDUCATION/EXPERIENCE Master of Arts, Interdisciplinary Arts, Columbia College (2002); Bachelor of Arts, Rhetoric, with a minor in Sociology & Video Production, University of Illinois at Urbana-Champaign (2000).

CURRENT STATUS Self-produced *Vida,* a CD of her poetry; pursuing a MAT degree in Education from National Louis University. Katherrine currently resides in Chicago, Illinois.

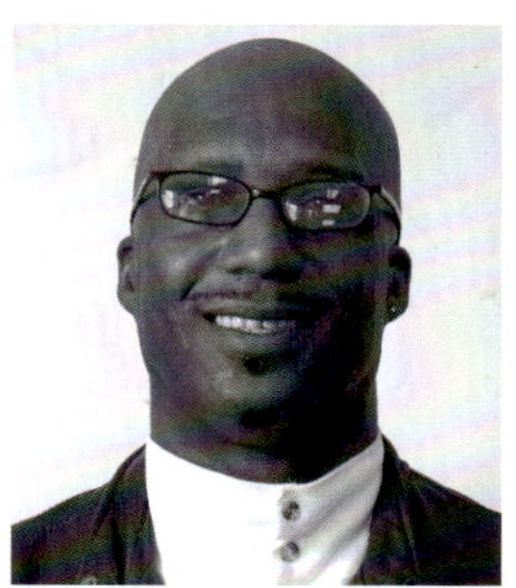

NAME Broadway, Steve

BORN Joliet, IL

EDUCATION/EXPERIENCE Undergraduate studies at Central University of Iowa; over 30 years of experience as a writer, poet, actor, songwriter.

CURRENT STATUS Actor, songwriter and music producer. Steve's latest project is a commemorative song celebrating the Chicago White Sox 2005 World Series Championship. As an actor, Steve has appeared as an extra and performed stunt work and stand-in on Fox TV series *Prison Break*, 20th Century Fox movies *Stranger Than Fiction*, *You're Going to Prison* and *Derailed.* Steve lives in Joliet with his wife and four children.

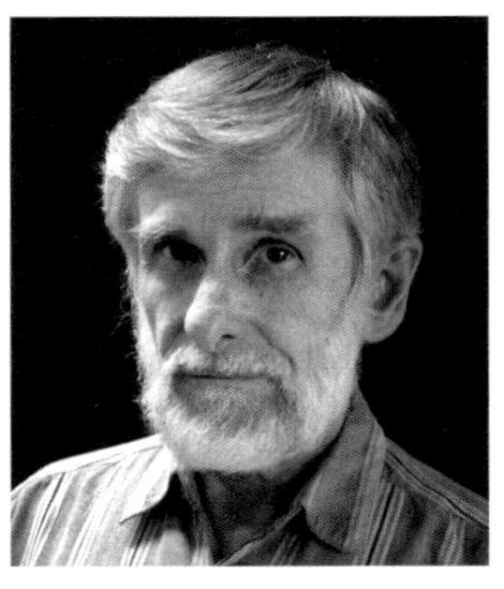

NAME Fischer, Earl Valentine

BORN Milwaukee, WI

EDUCATION/EXPERIENCE Bachelor of Arts, Journalism, with minor in Philosophy, Marquette University (1958)

CURRENT STATUS Retired Editor and Editorial Director, American Trade Magazines Division of Crain Communications, Inc. Chicago. Member of Illinois State Poetry Society and Joliet Drama Guild. Earl does personal performances of Samuel Taylor Coleridge's narrative poem, *The Rime of the Ancient Mariner.* Earl resides in Joliet with his wife Nancy.

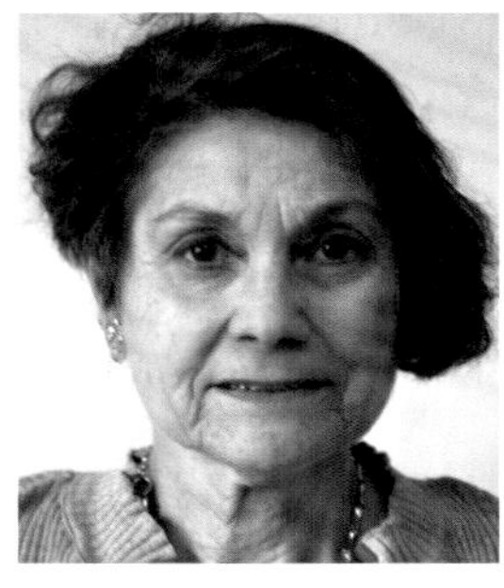

NAME Fischer, Nancy

BORN Evanston, IL

EDUCATION/EXPERIENCE Bachelor of Arts in Home Economics, Clothing and Textiles with minor in Education, Mundelein College (1980)

CURRENT STATUS Retired educator who is now engaging in numerous creative pursuits. Nancy resides in Joliet with her husband Earl.

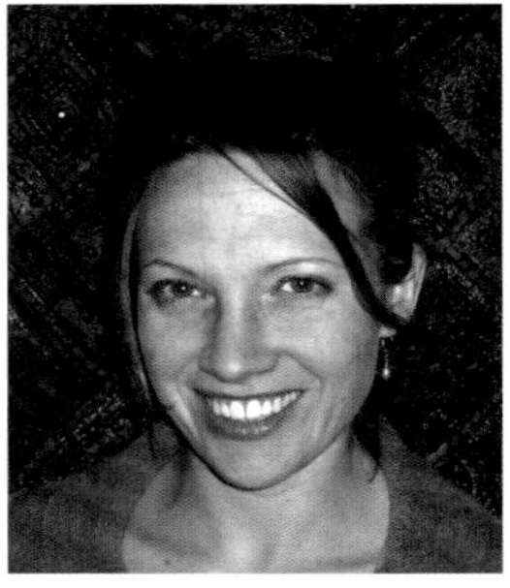

NAME Gillespie, Manda Aufochs

BORN Dayton, OH

EDUCATION/EXPERIENCE Master of Fine Arts in Writing, the School of the Art Institute of Chicago (2005); Bachelor of Art in Environmental Studies, Oberlin College (1998)

CURRENT STATUS Besides writing, Manda Aufochs Gillespie spends her days teaching poetry to kids and standing on her head. The day when she can do both simultaneously is timed to coincide with the publication of her first novel.

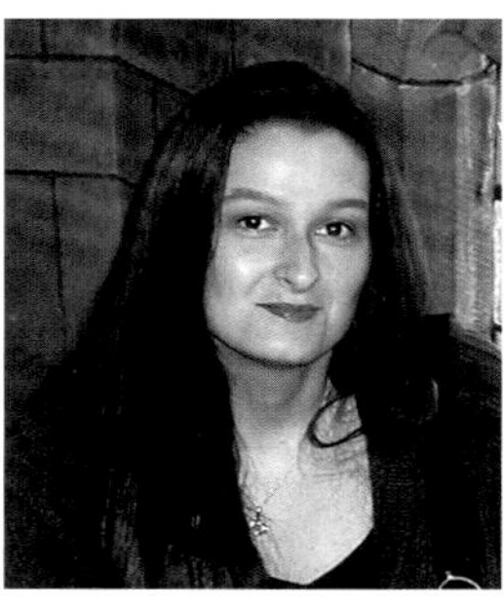

NAME Kurtz-Ogilvie, Whitney

BORN Danville, KY

EDUCATION/EXPERIENCE Master of Fine Arts in Creative Writing, the School of the Art Institute of Chicago (2005); Bachelor of Arts in English with Creative Writing Minor, University of Maryland Baltimore County (1999).

CURRENT STATUS Professor of English at Columbia College and currently writing her first novel. Whitney resides in Chicago with her husband and their three cats, Circe, Miete and Iselin.

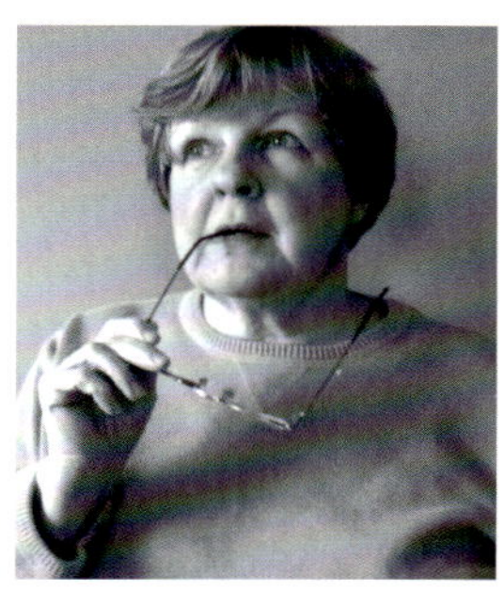

NAME Lockhart, Nancy

BORN Bayonne, NJ

EDUCATION/EXPERIENCE Bachelor of Arts in Elementary Education, College of St. Francis (1988); Associate in Arts and Science, Joliet Junior College (1982).

CURRENT STATUS Among her poetry achievements, Nancy has been awarded writing prizes in Durham, NC, Evanston, IL and Flint, MI. Nancy Lockhart had her own business partnership for a time, The Write Sister. She has taught pre-school, elementary students and adults. She is presently a "stay-at-home grandmother" and enjoys membership in two creative writing groups.

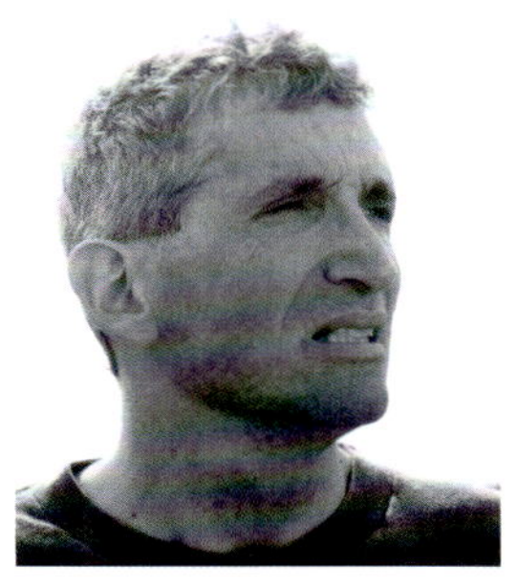

NAME Miller, George David

BORN Cumberland, MD

EDUCATION/EXPERIENCE Doctorate of Philosophy, DePaul University (1988); Master of Arts, Philosophy, Ohio University (1984); Bachelor of Science, Philosophy and English, Towson University (1981).

CURRENT STATUS Professor of Philosophy at Lewis University in Romeoville, Illinois; author of six books on philosophy and poetry. In 1997, The Carnegie Foundation for the Advancement of Teaching named him Illinois Professor of the Year. As the founder and President of Before I Read This Poem, Inc., George performs and facilities poetry workshops at elementary, junior high, high schools and colleges.

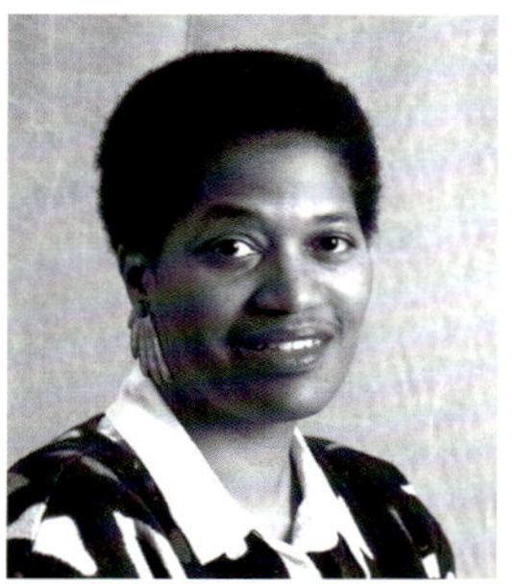

NAME Mitchell, Gwendolyn

BORN Pittsburgh, PA

EDUCATION/EXPERIENCE Master of Fine Arts, English: Poetry, Pennsylvania State University (1991); Bachelor of Arts, Political Science, Pennsylvania State University (1988)

CURRENT STATUS Serves as the Senior Editor at Third World Press Publishing Company in Chicago, IL. Published works include *House of Women,* 2002; *Veins and Rivers: A Book of Ten Poems*, 1998; *Ain't I Black* 2004; *Releasing the Spirit: A Collection of Literary Works from Gallery 37* (Coeditor with Haki R. Madhubuti), 1998; *Describe the Moment: A Collection of Literary Works from Gallery 37* (Coeditor with Haki R. Madhubuti) 2000. Gwendolyn resides in Chicago, Illinois

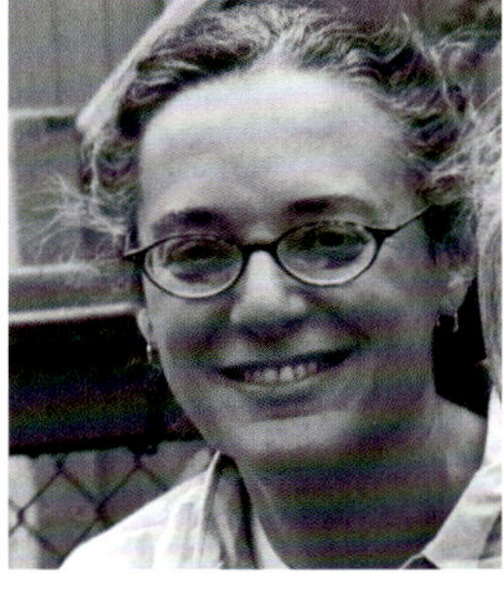

NAME Parson-Nesbitt, Julie

BORN Chicago, IL

EDUCATION/EXPERIENCE Master of Fine Arts, Creative Writing University of Pittsburgh (1996); Bachelor of Arts, Chinese Language and Literature, University of Wisconsin-Madison (1980).

CURRENT STATUS Author of the poetry collection *Finders* (West End Press); coeditor of *Power Lines: A Decade of Poetry from Chicago's Guild Complex* (Tia Chucha Press) and *Naming Daytime Moon: Stories and Poems by Chicago Women.* Julie is currently the Development Director for Young Chicago Authors, a nonprofit organization that encourages creative writing among teens. She was previously Executive Director of the Guild Complex, a cross-cultural literary arts center. She lives in Chicago, Illinois.

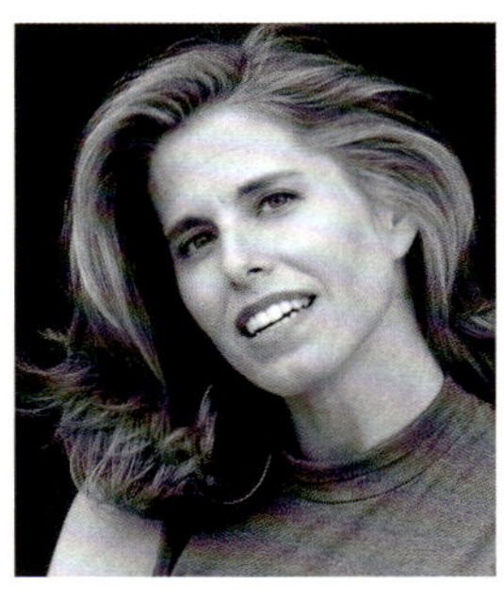

NAME Paschen, Elise

BORN Chicago, IL

EDUCATION/EXPERIENCE Doctorate of Philosophy, English Studies, Twentieth Century Literature, Oxford University (1988); Master of Arts, English Studies, Twentieth Century Literature, Oxford University (1984); Bachelor of Arts, English and American Literature, Harvard University (1982).

CURRENT STATUS Professor, Writing Program at the School of the Art Institute of Chicago. Work includes *Infidelities*, winner of the Nicholas Roerich Poetry Prize, published by Story Line Press; editor of *Poetry Speaks to Children*, coeditor of *Poetry Speaks*, *Poetry in Motion*, and *Poetry in Motion from Coast to Coast*. Poems published in magazines such as *Poetry*, *The New Yorker*, *The New Republic*, and in numerous anthologies. Elise lives in Chicago, Illinois.

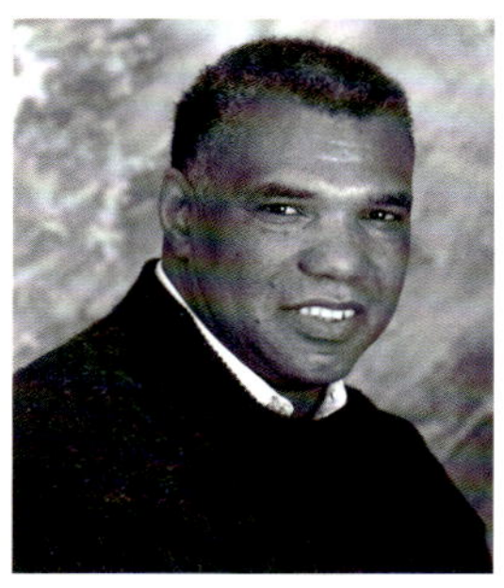

NAME Plumpp, Sterling D.

BORN Clinton, MS

EDUCATION/EXPERIENCE Graduate studies, Roosevelt University; Bachelor of Arts, Psychology, Roosevelt University (1968)

CURRENT STATUS Professor Emeritus, University of Illinois, Chicago, where he serves on the faculty in the African American Studies and English Departments. Currently teaches in the Master of Fine Arts Program, Chicago State University. *Portable Soul, Half Black, Half Blacker*, and *Steps to Break to the Circle* are only some his numerous published works. Sterling resides in Chicago, Illinois.

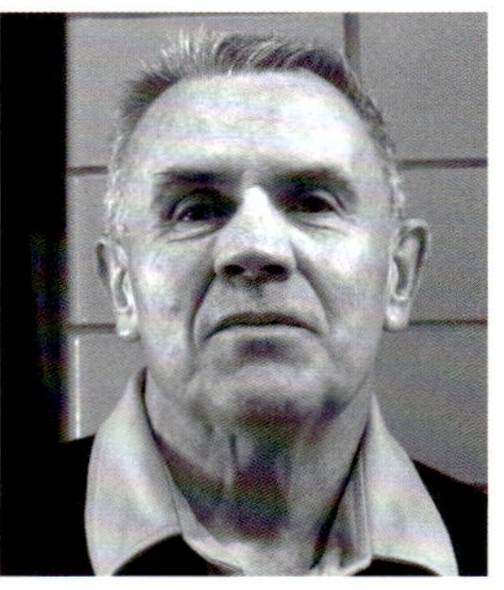

NAME Stobart, John

BORN Harrisburg, IL

EDUCATION/EXPERIENCE Master of Arts, English, Southern Illinois University (1961); Bachelor of Arts, English with minors in Education, History, Psychology, Southern Illinois University (1958).

CURRENT STATUS Retired in 1999 from Joliet Junior College, where he taught Creative Writing, Contemporary Literature, American Literature, British Literature, and English for 39 years and he was the sponsor of JJC Literary Magazine for 26 years. John resides in Joliet, Illinois.

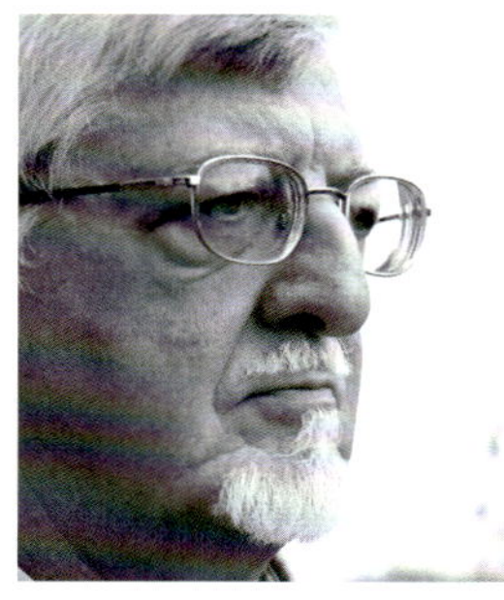

NAME Thompson, Ted

BORN Bloomington, IN

EDUCATION/EXPERIENCE Master of Arts, English, University of Chicago (1967); Bachelor of Arts, English, Indiana University (1965); Professor of English, Joliet Junior College 1967–2003.

CURRENT STATUS Semi retired from teaching literature and film courses at Joliet Junior College and from teaching an on-line writing course, Writing Prose and Poetry, at the University of St. Francis. Ted resides in Joliet, Illinois.

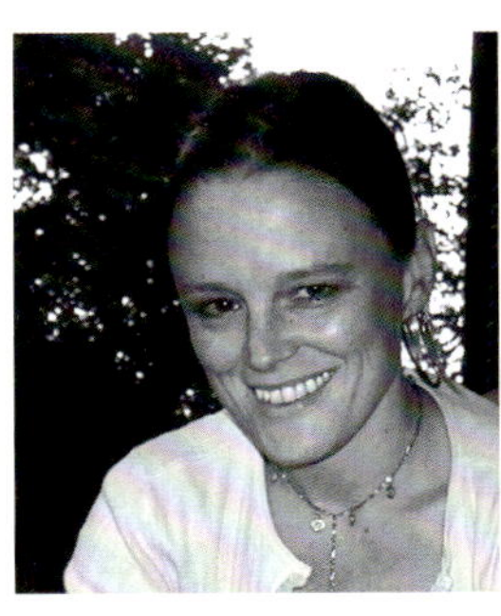

NAME Vollmer-Lawson, Kim

BORN Joliet, IL

EDUCATION/EXPERIENCE Master of Fine Arts, Poetry, Western Michigan University (1999); Bachelor of Arts, Rhetoric, University of Illinois (1994); Associate of Arts, General Education, Joliet Junior College (1989).

CURRENT STATUS Mother of two, lover of sunshine and trees; Professor of Literature, Composition, and Creative Writing, University of St. Francis. Kim resides in Joliet, Illinois.

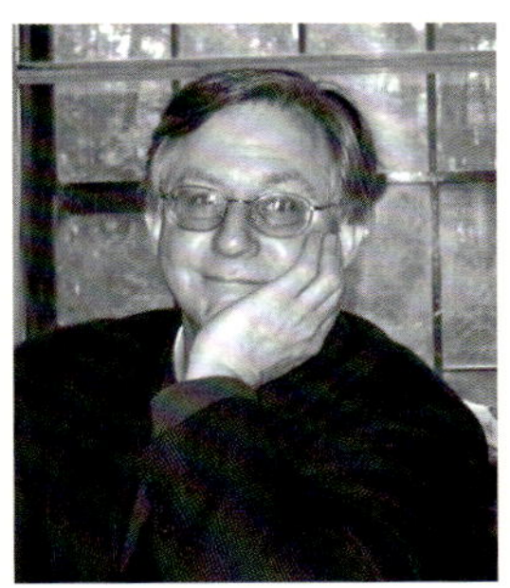

NAME Yarrow, William

BORN Philadelphia, PA

EDUCATION/EXPERIENCE Master of Arts, English Literature, Northwestern University, (1976); Bachelor of Arts, English Literature, Swarthmore College (1973).

CURRENT STATUS Poems have appeared in *The Antigonish Review, Berkeley Poets Cooperative, Central Park, Confrontation, DuPage ArtsLife, Hazotzer, The Literary Review, Midstream, Muse Apprentice Guild*, and *Poem*. Bill is Professor of English at Joliet Junior College.

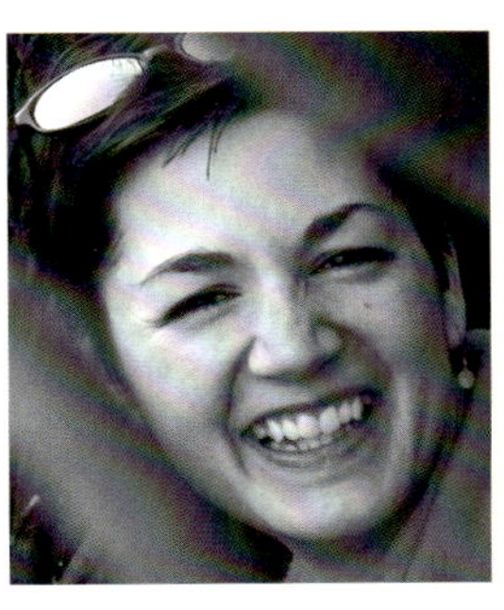

NAME Wallace, Valerie Martt

BORN Sacramento, California

EDUCATION/EXPERIENCE Master of Fine Arts, Writing, the Art Institute of Chicago (2005); Bachelor of Arts, Psychology, Bethany College (1990)

CURRENT STATUS Published in *Rhino Magazine, Maize, Borderlands: Texas Poetry Review, Midwest Poetry Review,* and other journals. Valerie lives in Chicago, Illinois, where she is Administrative Director of Urban Life Center, a nontraditional college program.

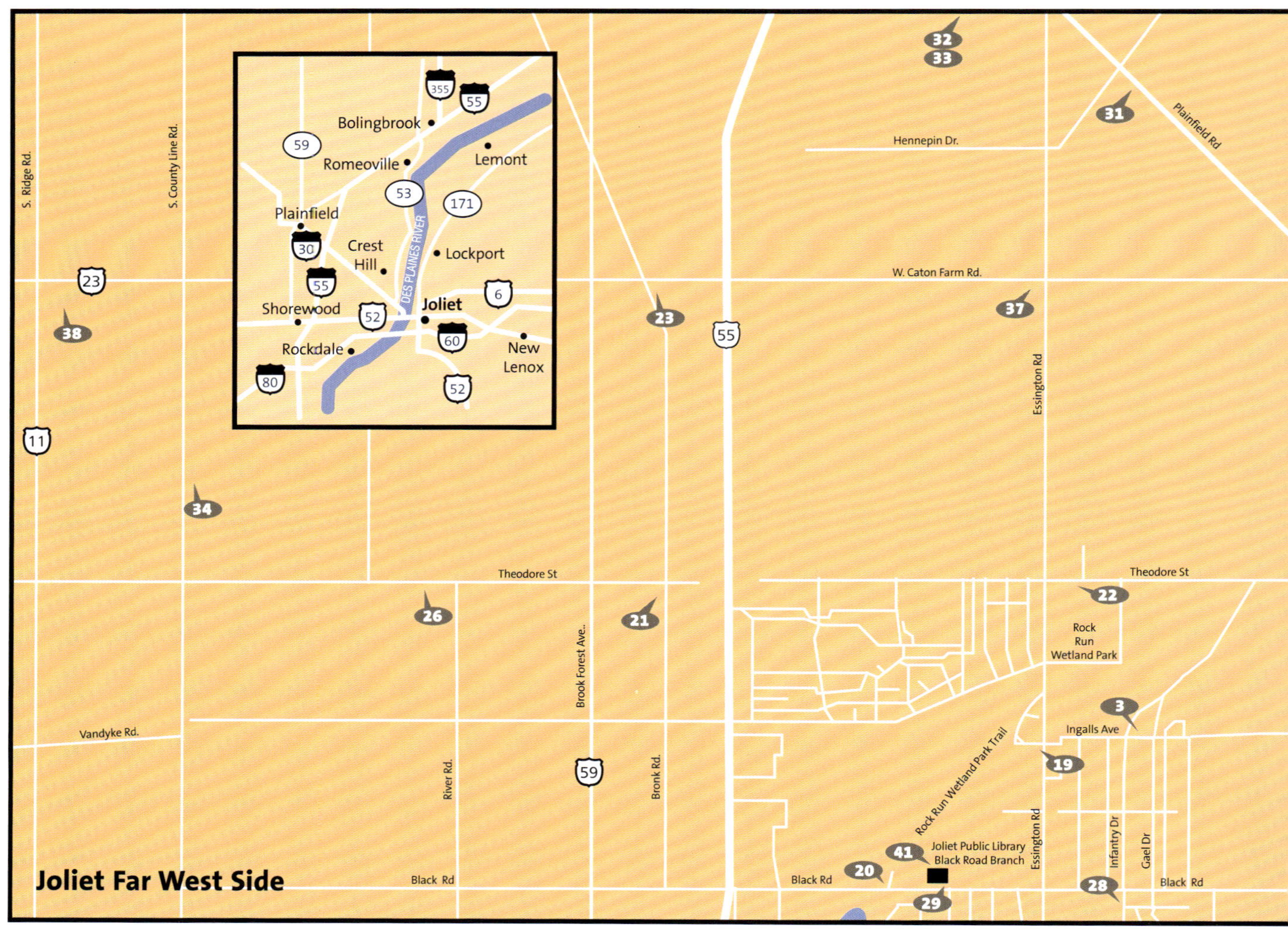

Sculptures and Locations

Dimensions are height x width x depth

1. **Building the Lincoln Highway** (2005)
Cold-cast bronze sculpture, 6' x 2.5' x 4'
1600 Plainfield Rd., Joliet

2. **Route 66: The Mother Road** (2006)
Cold-cast bronze sculpture, 6' x 3' x 2'
200-204 N. Ottawa St., Joliet.

3. **Veteran Women: Proudly They Serve**
Cold-cast bronze sculpture, 4' x 2' x 2.5'
American Legion Post 1080
2625 Ingalls Ave., Joliet

4. **Sator Sanchez: World War II Hero** (2000)
Cold-cast bronze sculpture, 8' x 4' x 2.5'
Corner of Collins St. & Ohio St., Joliet

5. **Katherine Dunham: Dancer, Choreographer and Citizen** (2001)
Cold-cast bronze sculpture, 7' x 3' x 2'
Union Station, Jefferson & Scott Sts., Joliet

6. **George Mikan: Changed the Game of Basketball Forever** (2006)
Hot-cast bronze sculpture,
7'10"H x 3' 5" x 2' 7"
Corner of Broadway St. (George Mikan Blvd.) & Ingalls Ave., Joliet

7. **Jesse Barfield: A Great Joliet Baseball Tradition** (2003)
Hot-cast bronze sculpture, 7.5' x 3' x 2'
1 Arthur Schultz Dr. (Silver Cross Field), Joliet

8. **Community Policing: Working with Citizens for a Safer City** (2004)
Hand-carved limestone sculpture,
5'4" x 2'4" x 3'
470 N. Chicago St., Joliet

9. **Joliet Fire Fighters: Helping Hands, Caring Hearts** (2003)
Cold-cast bronze sculpture, 8' x 3' x 2.5'
Corner of Jackson St. & Garnsey Ave., Joliet

10. **Monarch of the Prairie** (2003)
Cold-cast bronze sculpture, 4' x 5' x 2'
Northwest corner of Raynor Ave. & Plainfield Rd., Joliet

11. **Asakiwaki Woman** (2002)
Cold-cast bronze sculpture,
6' x 1'6" x 1'6 "
Southwest corner of Raynor Ave. & Plainfield Rd., Joliet

12. **The First Pioneer** (2005)
Cold-cast bronze sculpture, 6' x 2' x 3'
Corner of Washington & Richards Sts., Joliet

13. **1850s Barber: Underground Railroad Hero** (2002)
Cold-cast bronze sculpture, 4' x 2' x 1.5'
Northwest corner of S. Chicago & McDonough Sts., Joliet

14. **Traveling the Plank Road: A Working Companionship** (2002)
Cold-cast bronze sculpture, 3' x 2' x 2'
Northwest corner of Plainfield Rd. & Ingalls Ave., Joliet

15. **History Clings like Ivy** (2003)
Cold-cast bronze sculpture, 5' x 3' x 2'
Corner of Raynor & Western Aves., Joliet

16. **Historic Preservation: Our Neighborhood** (2000)
Cold-cast bronze sculpture, 4' x 10" x 10"
Preservation Park, Wilcox St. & Glenwood Ave., Joliet

17. **Portals of Buell Avenue** (2002)
Two powder-coated steel sculptures,
14' x 10'; 16' x 10'
Corner of Center St. & Western Ave., Joliet

18. **The New Steelman** (2000)
Cor-ten steel Sculpture, 8' x 4' x 1"
Joliet Township High School Central Campus, E. Jefferson St. & Eastern Ave., Joliet

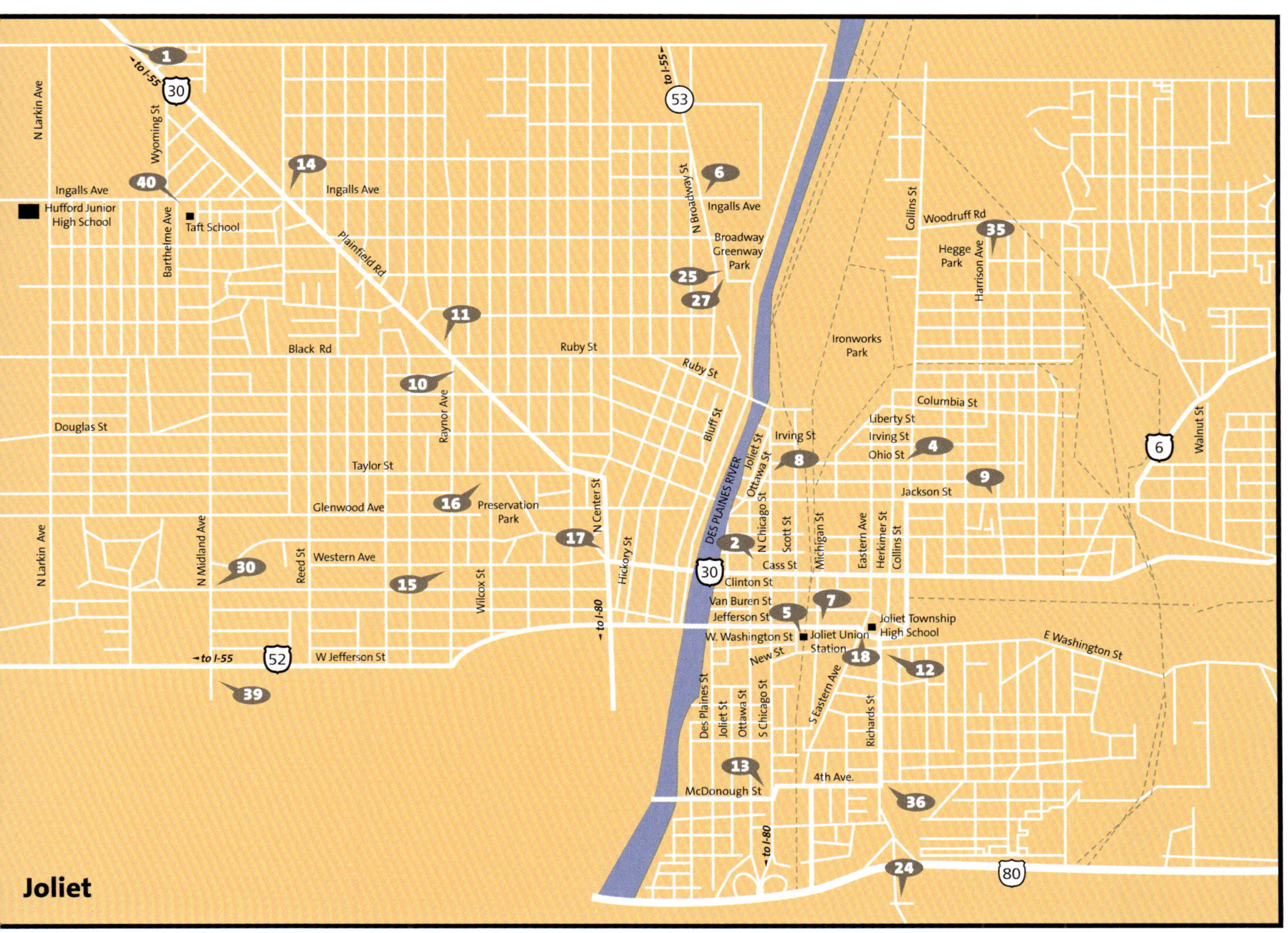

19. **Egrets in the Wetland** (1998)
Faux stone sculpture, 4' x 2.5' x 2'
Essington Rd. at Ingalls Ave., Joliet

20. **The Barn Owl and the Moon** (2000)
Faux stone sculpture, 4' x 2' x 2'
Rock Run Wetland Park, bike path on Black Rd., Joliet

21. **Red Tail Hawk: The Nature of Our Neighborhood** (2002)
Cold-cast bronze sculpture, 2.5' x 3.5' x 2'
Corner of Theodore & Mallard Sts., Joliet

22. **Fox in Cattails** (2003)
Cold-cast bronze sculpture, 3' x 3' x 2.5'
Corner of Theodore & DelRose Sts., Joliet

23. **Nature: The Flow of Life** (2006)
Cold-cast bronze sculpture, 3'8" x 20" x 2'
Caton Farm Rd. at the DuPage River, Joliet

24. **Wisdom: A Grandmother and Grandchild** (2003)
Cold-cast bronze sculpture, 5' x 4' x 3'
Sunny Hill Skilled Rehab Center, 421 Doris Ave., Joliet

25. **Mother Nature** (1999)
Cold-cast bronze sculpture, 4' x 4' x 2'
Broadway Greenway Park, Broadway St., Joliet

26. **Tiller of the Earth** (2002)
Cold-cast bronze sculpture, 6' x 5' x 2.5'
Troy Middle School, 5800 Theodore St., Joliet

27. **Spirit of the River** (2002)
Cold-cast bronze sculpture, 5' x 6.5' x 2'
Broadway Greenway Park, Broadway St., Joliet

28. **The Boy and the Rose** (2000)
Cold-cast bronze sculpture, 5' x 4' x 2'
539 N. Infantry Dr. near Black Rd., Joliet

29. **An Informed Mind Can Make Better Choices** (2001)
Cold-cast bronze sculpture, 5.5' x 2.5' x 2'
Joliet Public Library West Branch, 3395 W. Black Rd., Joliet

30. **Justice** (2006)
Cold-cast bronze sculpture, 6' x 3' x 3'
250 N. Midland Ave., Joliet

31. **Ebb and Flow** (2006)
Cold-cast bronze sculpture 6' x 3' x 3'
Hennepin Dr. at Plainfield Rd. (Rt. 30), Joliet

32. **The New Dress** (2001)
Cold-cast bronze sculpture with powder coated steel base, 3' x 1' x 1.5'
Inside Westfield Louis Joliet Mall, 3340 Mall Loop Dr., Joliet

33. **The Gift of Music** (2001)
Cold-cast bronze sculpture with powder coated steel base, 3'5" x 1'6" x 1'6"
Inside Westfield Louis Joliet Mall, 3340 Mall Loop Dr., Joliet

34. **I Wonder** (2003)
Cold-cast bronze sculpture, 5' x 3' x 2'
Meadowview Elementary School, 2501 Mirage Ave., Joliet

35. **A Teacher's Gift** (2003)
Cold-cast bronze sculpture, 5' x 4' x 3'
Sator Sanchez Elementary School, 1101 Harrison Ave., Joliet

36. **High Expectations** (2002)
Cold-cast bronze sculpture, 3' x 2' x 2'
Washington Jr. High School, 402 Richards St., Joliet

37. **The Creative Spirit Soars** (2004)
Cold-cast bronze sculpture, 5' x 4' x 3'
Grand Prairie Elementary School, 3300 Caton Farm Rd., Joliet

38. **Reaching for Our Destinies** (2004)
Cold-cast bronze sculpture, 5' x 6' x 2'
Plainfield South High School, 7800 W. Caton Farm Rd., Joliet

39. **Education Is the Window to the World** (2003)
Cold-cast bronze sculpture, 5' x 3' x 2'
Dirksen Jr. High School, 203 S. Midland Ave., Joliet

40. **Planting the Seeds: Children and Education** (1999)
Cold-cast bronze sculpture, 4' x 4' x 2'
Taft School, 1125 N. Oregon St. near Ingalls Ave., Joliet

41. **Alice: Phyllis Reynolds Naylor's Young Heroine** (2001)
Cold-cast bronze sculpture, 3' x 4' x 3.5'
Joliet Public Library West Branch, 3395 West Black Rd., Joliet

mosaic columns

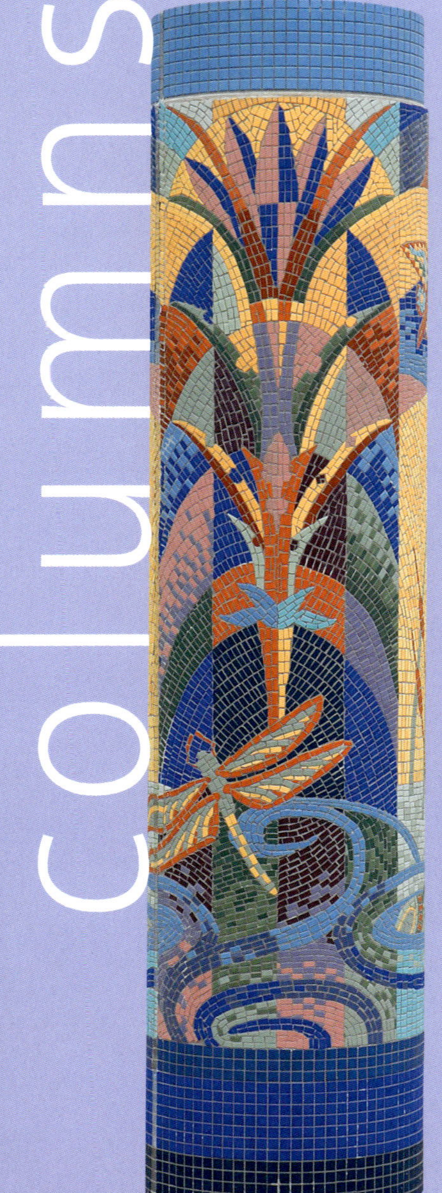

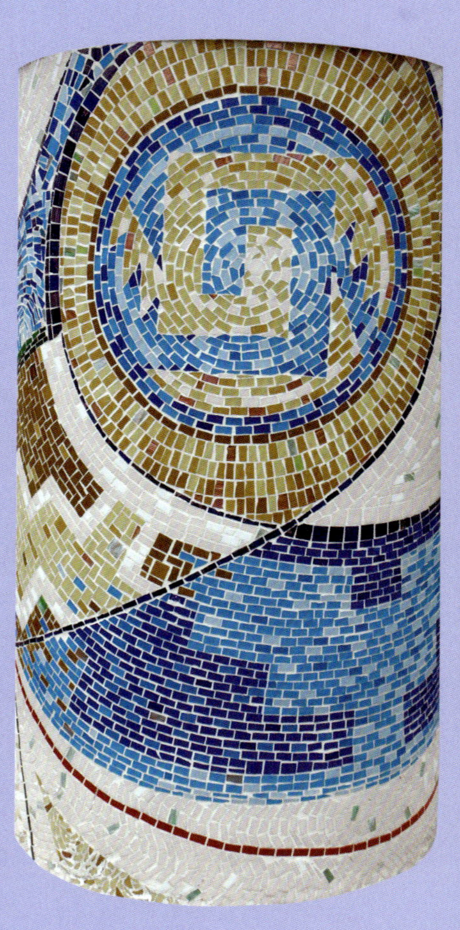

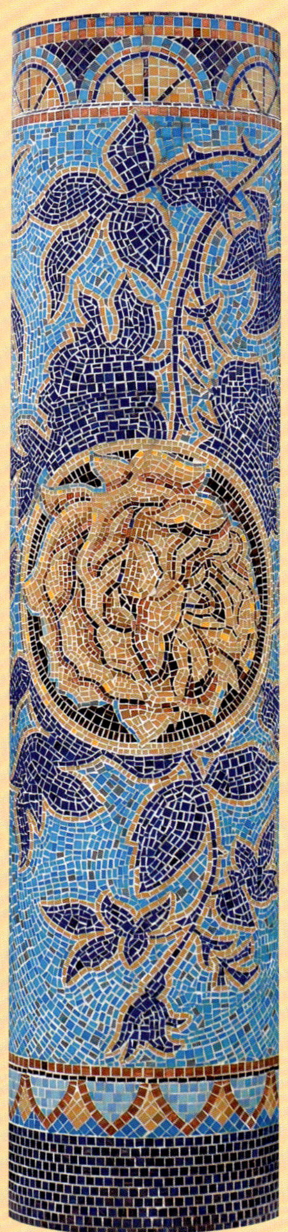

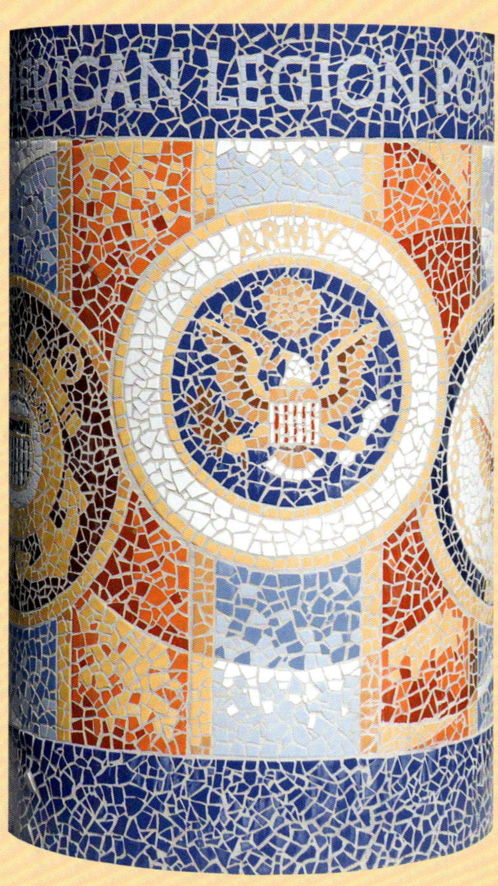

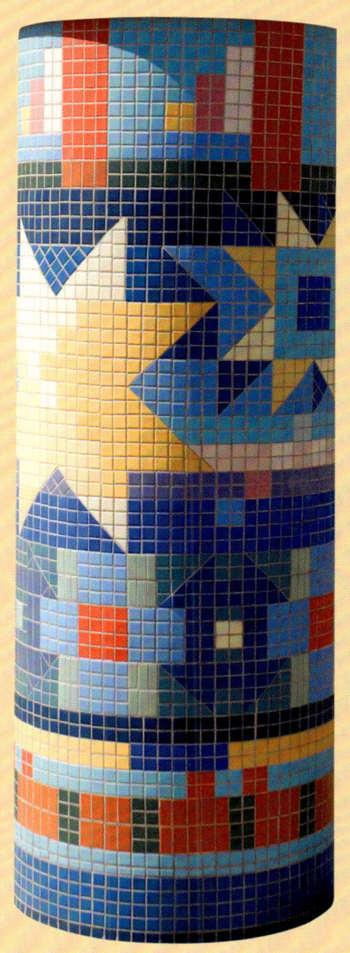

MOSAIC ARTISTS
Left to right

27 *Spirit of the River*, Saul Chavira

19 *Egrets in the Wetland*, Kathleen Scarboro

4 *Sator Sanchez: WW II Hero*, Ilario Silva

28 *The Boy & the Rose*, Andrea Rountree

3 *Veteran Women*, Dante DiBartolo

13 *1850s Barber*, Kreshaun McKinney

Selected Resource Guide

Public Art Internet Sites

Public Art on the Net: www.zpub.com/public

Public Monuments & Sculpture Association: www.pmsa.org.uk

Online resource for public art information and documentation: www.art-public.com

Forecast Public Artworks: www.forecastart.org

Public Art Review (periodical); www.publicartreview.org

Public Art Research Archive: public-art.shu.ac.uk

Public Art Fund: www.publicartfund.org

Public Art Online: www.publicartonline.org.uk

Public Art in LA: www.publicartinla.com

Public Art in Downtown Cincinnati: www.idiotech.com/oacdocs/oachome.html

Philadelphia Public Art: www.philart.net

Art in Public Places (Miami): www.miamidade.gov/publicart

Americans for the Arts: www.americansforthearts.org

Friends of Community Public Art (Joliet, Il.): www.fcpaonline.org

Figurative Sculpture Organizations

National Sculpture Society: www.nationalsculpture.org

The Society of Portrait Sculptors: www.portrait-sculpture.org

Sculpture Books (technique):

Modeling a Likeness in Clay, Daisy Grubbs,Watson-Guptill Publications, New York, 1982

Modeling the Figure in Clay, Bruno Lucchesi and Margit Malmstrom,Watson-Guptill Publications, New York, 1980

Modeling the Head in Clay, Bruno Lucchesi and Margit Malmstrom, Watson-Guptill Publications, New York, 1979

The Clay Modeling Handbook, Mario Molteni, Clarkson N. Potter, Inc. publisher, New York, 1992

From Clay to Bronze, Tuck Langland, Watson-Guptill Publications, New York, 1999

The Technique of Casting for Sculpture, John W. Mills, Publisher B. T. Batsford Ltd., London, 1990

Terracotta, Bruno Lucchesi and Margit Malmstrom, Watson-Guptill Publications, New York, 1977

Figure Sculpture in Wax and Plaster, Richard McDermott Miller, Dover Publications, Mineola, N. Y., 1971

Sculpture Supplies:

The Compleat Sculptor, 800-9-SCULPT, www.sculpt.com

Sculpture House, 609-466-2986, sculpturehouse.com

Trow & Holden Stone Cutting tools, 802-476-7221, 800-451-4349, www.trowandholden.com

Plasticine Clay: J.F. McCaughin Co., 626-573-3000

Mold Makers, Casters

Mold maker, caster in resin: AFS LTD, 4401 S. Western Blvd, Chicago, Il 60609

Mold maker, caster in bronze: Jeff Adams' in Bronze Studio/Gallery/Foundry, 815-734-7578, www.inbronze.com, 309 N. Wesley Ave., Mount Morris, IL 61054

Mosaic Books

Pebble Mosaics, Maggy Howarth, Search Press Limited, New Zealand, 1994

Handmade Tiles, Frank Giorgini, Lark Books, Asheville, NC, 1994

Mosaic Supplies

Outdoor porcelain ceramic and glass tile

Bisazza "vetricolor" and "le gemme" glass tile: www.bisazzausa.com, Brann Clay Products, 708 422 1000, 12430 S. Kedvale Ave., Alsip, Il 60803

Daltile "keystones", "permatones" and "permabrites" (porcelain) tile, also "kolorines" Venetian Glass Mosaic tiles: Daltile, 630 789 1400, www.daltile.com, PO Box 70671, Chicago, Il. 60673-0671

American Olean unglazed ceramic mosaic tile: www.americanolean.com, American Olean Midwest, 847 238 9780, 805 Mark Street, Elk Grove Village, Il. 60007

Can-Do polyfilm tape #358: Can-Do National Tape, 615 255 1775, 800 643 5996, 195 Polk Ave., Nashville, TN, 37210

Index

Artists, Assistant Artists, Poets, and Subjects of Sculptures, (Bold number denotes large photograph of sculptures)

African-American: The Story of Katherine Dunham 23; Katherine Dunham: Dancer, Choreographer and Citizen 24, **25**; *Madame Dunham 24*; *Jesse Barfield:* A Great Joliet Baseball Tradition **28**, 29; *Joliet's Jesse 29*; The First Pioneer 38, **39**; *Progressive Pioneer 38*; 1850s Barber: Underground Railroad Hero **40**, 41, 109; *Together From the Start 41*.

Allegory: Wisdom: A Grandmother and Grandchild 62, **63**; *Touching 62;* Mother Nature **64**, 65 *Cold Spring 65*; The Tiller of the Earth 66, **67**; *The Tiller of the Earth 66;* Spirit of the River **68**, 69, 109*; Spirit Sonnet 69*; The Boy and the Rose 70, **71**, 109; *By Any Other Name 70*; An Informed Mind Can Make Better Choices **72**, 73; *An Informed Mind 73;* Justice **74** *Conviction 75;* Ebb and Flow 76, **77**; *Think Even This 76*; The New Dress **78**, 79; *"The New Dress" 79;* the Gift of Music 80, **81**; *New Horn 80*.

Architecture: History Clings Like Ivy 44, **45**; *Cathedral Area 44*; Historic Preservation: Our Neighborhood **46**, 47; *Rejuvenation 47*; Portals of Buell Avenue 48, **49**; *Dark Good Memories 48*.

Armature, 9.

Bailly, Annick, 28, 68, 72, 74.

Barber: 1850s Barber: Underground Railroad Hero **40**, 41,109;*Together From the Start 41*.

Bardales, Katherinne, 24, 101 (bio).

Barfield, Jesse **28**, 29.

Baseball: Jesse Barfield: A Great Joliet Baseball Tradition **28**, 29; *Joliet's Jesse 29*.

Basketball: George Mikan: Changed the Game of Basketball for Forever 26, **27**;*Goaltender 26*.

Bison: Monarch of the Prairie 34, **35**; *The Bison's Alimony 34*.

Broadway, Steve, 29, 101 (bio).

Carlson, Roger, 21, 25, 45, 46, 72, 96.

Cathedral Area; History Clings Like Ivy 44, **45**; *Cathedral Area 44*; Historic Preservation: Our Neighborhood **46**, 47; *Rejuvenation 47*; Portals of Buell Avenue 48, **49**; *Dark Good Memories 48*.

Chavira, Saul, 21, 28, 40, 43, 63, 68, 100 (bio).

Clay, 9.

Cold cast bronze, 9.

Community Policing, 30, **31**.

Conservation 76, **77**; *Think Even This 76*.

Construction: Building the Lincoln Highway 14, **15**; *Concrete Rivers 14*; Route 66: The Mother Road 16, **17**; *Route 66 16*.

Dance: The Story of Katherine Dunham 23; Katherine Dunham: Dancer, Choreographer and Citizen 24, **25**; *Madame Dunham 24*.

DiBartolo, Dante,9,15, 18, 21, 25, 27, 28, 32, 35, 40, 43, 45, 46, 53, 55, 56, 64, 67, 68, 71, 72, 74, 81, 87, 91, 95, 96, 99 (bio).

Diversity: A Teacher's Gift (Sator Sanchez Elementary School) **84**, 85; *Bombardier Martyrdom 85*; High Expectations 86, **87**; *High Expectations 86*.

Dirksen Jr. High School, 92.

Dunham, Katherine, 23, 24, **25**.

Education: I Wonder (Meadowview Elementary School) 82, **83**; *I Wonder 82*; A Teacher's Gift (Sator Sanchez Elementary School) **84**; *Bombardier Martyrdom 85*; High Expectations (Washington Jr. High School) 86, **87**; *High Expectations 86*; The Creative Spirit Soars (Grand Prairie Elementary School) **88**, 89; *The Ponder Bird 89*; Reaching for Our Destinies (Plainfield South High School) 90, **91**; *Reaching for our Destinies 90*; Education is the Window to the World (Dirksen Jr. High School) **92**, 93; *March Madness: Intergalactic League 93*; Planting the Seeds: Children and Education (Taft Elementary School) 94, **95**; *Child Guide 94*.

Egrets: Egrets in the Wetland 52, **53**, 108; *Egret 52*.

Farming: The Tiller of the Earth 66, **67**; *The Tiller of the Earth 66*.

Farrell, Kathleen, 8, 15, 21, 25, 28, 32, 40, 53, 64, 68, 71, 72, 74, 81, 98 (bio).

Faulhaber, Roberta, 15.

Fire Fighting: Joliet Fire Fighters: Helping Hands, Caring Hearts **32**, 33; *Firefighter 33*.

Fischer, Earl Valentine, 38, 48, 58, 102 (bio).

Fischer, Nancy 61, 102.

Fox: Fox in Cattails 58, **59**; *Hail, Splendidissima! 58*.

Furst, Sarah, 25, 35, 40, 55, 56, 59, 60, 63, 64, 71, 77, 81, 88, 98 (bio).

Gillespie, Manda Aufochs 76, 102.

Glet, Sharka, 9, 15, 17, 28, 32, 77, 92, 98 (bio).

Grand Prairie Elementary School Students, 88.

Hawk: Red Tail Hawk: The Nature of Our Neighborhood **56**, 57; *The Hawk 57*.

History: Building the Lincoln Highway 14, **15**; *Concrete Rivers 14;* Route 66: The Mother Road 16, **17**; *Route 66 16*; Veteran Women: Proudly They Serve **18**,19, 109; *Joliet's Female Veterans 19;* Sator Sanchez: World War II Hero

20, **21**, 108; *Sandy Sanchez 20* ; The Story of Sator Sanchez 22; The Story of Katherine Dunham 23; Katherine Dunham: Dancer, Choreographer and Citizen 24, **25**; *Madame Dunham 24*; George Mikan: *Changed the Game of Basketball Forever* 26, **27**; *Goaltender 26*; Jesse Barfield: A Great Joliet Baseball Tradition **28**, 29; *Joliet's Jesse 29*;Community Policing: Working with Citizens for a Safer City 30, **31**; *A Policeman is the Semaphore of Civilization 30*; Joliet Fire Fighters: Helping Hands, Caring Hearts **32**, 33; *Firefighter 33*; Monarch of the Prairie 34, **35**; *The Bison's Alimony 34;* Asakiwaki Woman **36**;*They Endured 37*; The First Pioneer 38, **39**; *Progressive Pioneer 38*; 1850s Barber: Underground Railroad Hero **40**, 41, 109; *Together From the Start 41*; Traveling the Plank Road: A Working Companionship 42, **43**; *Founding Father 42;* History Clings Like Ivy 44, **45**; *Cathedral Area 44*; Historic Preservation: Our Neighborhood **46**, 47; *Rejuvenation 47*; Portals of Buell Avenue 48, **49**; *Dark Good Memories 48*; The New Steelman **50**; *Steelman 2006, 51.*

Horse: Traveling the Plank Road: A Working Companionship 42, **43**; *Founding Father 42*

Jackson, Share, 17.

Kurtz-Ogilvie, Whitney, 75, 102 (bio).

Lega, Marsha, 49, 50, 78, 81, 98 (bio).

Lincoln Highway: 14, 15.

Lockhart, Nancy, 80, 82, 103 (bio).

McKinney, Kreshaun, 40, 87, 100 (bio).

Meadowview Elementary School, 83.

Mexican-American: Sator Sanchez: World War II Hero 20, 21, 108; *Sandy Sanchez 20*; *the Story of Sator Sanchez 22.*

Mikan, George, 26, **27**; *Goaltender 26.*

Miller, George David, 14, 20, 33, 86, 90, 103 (bio).

Mitchell, Gwendolyn, 79, 103 (bio).

Music: the Gift of Music 80, **81**; *New Horn 80.*

Native American: Asakiwaki Woman **36**, 37; *They Endured 37.*

Nature: Egrets in the Wetland 52, **53**, 108; *Egret 52*; The Barn Owl and the Moon 54, **55**; *The Barn Owl and the Moon 54*; Red Tail Hawk: The Nature of Our Neighborhood **56**, 57; *The Hawk 57*; Fox in Cattails 58, **59**; *Hail, Splendidissima! 58;* Nature: The Flow of Life 60, **61**; *The Flow 61.*

Naylor, Phyllis Reynolds, 96, 97.

Otter, Nature: The Flow of Life 60, **61**; *The Flow 61.*

Outland, Amy, 57.

Owl: The Barn Owl and the Moon 54, **55**; *The Barn Owl and the Moon 54.*

Parson-Nesbitt, Julie, 65, 103 (bio).

Paschen, Elise, 54, 104 (bio).

Plainfield South High School Art Students, 91.

Plumpp, Sterling, 66, 104 (bio).

Reading: An Informed Mind Can Make Better Choices **72**, 73; *An Informed Mind 73.* Alice: Phyllis Reynolds Naylor's Young Heroine **96**, 97; *Alice on a Book 97;*

Reyes-Albright, Denise, 91, 100.

Rodriguez, Jesus, 18, 31, 39, 84, 98 (bio).

Rountree, Andrea, 21, 64, 71, 100 (bio).

Route 30, 14, **15.**

Route 66, 16, **17.**

River: Spirit of the River, **68**, 69, 108.

Sanchez, Sator, 20, **21**, 22, 109.

Sator Sanchez Elementary School, 84.

Sauer, Emile, 15.

Scarboro, Kathleen, 10, 17, 36, 43, 45, 46, 53, 55, 67, 77, 78, 83, 87, 91, 95, 96, 99 (bio).

Silva, Ilario, 74, 74, 101 (bio).

Standifer, David, 9, 27, 74, 99 (bio).

Steelman: The New Steelman **50**, 51; *Steelman 2006, 51.*

Steel Sculpture: Portals of Buell Avenue **49**; *Dark Good Memories 48*; The New Steelman **50**, 51; *Steelman 2006, 51.*

Stobart, John, 12, 19, 37, 44, 51, 62, 85, 93, 97, 104 (bio).

Taft Elementary School, 95.

Thompson, Ted, 16, 42, 52, 70, 89, 104 (bio).

Underground Railroad: 1850s Barber: Underground Railroad Hero **40**, 41, 109; *Together From the Start 41.*

Veteran: Sator Sanchez: Veteran Women: Proudly They Serve **18**, 19, 109; *Joliet's Female Veterans 19.* World War II Hero 20, **21**, 109; the Story of Sator Sanchez 22; Vollmer—Lawson, Kim, 41, 47, 69, 94, 105 (bio).

Wallace, Valerie Martt 26, 105 (bio).

Washington Jr. High School, 87.

Wetland: Egrets in the Wetland 52, **53**; *Egret 52.*

Yadura-Gallaher, Kelly, 67, 92, 99 (bio).

Yanchick, David, 15, 17, 45, 67, 101 (bio).

Yarrow, William Paul 30, 34, 105 (bio).